From the pages of
THE WEEK

The World's Best Books

Edited by Mark Williams

Contents

First published in Great Britain in November 2006 by Dennis Publishing
30 Cleveland Street, London W1T 4JD

© 2006 Dennis Publishing Ltd

A CIP catalogue record for this book is available from the British Library.

ISBN 0 9516709 8 0

Designed by Andrew Riley
Jacket Design by Etienne Gilfillan
Cover Illustration by Paul Slater

Printed and Bound in India by International Print-o-Pac Ltd

Trade Distribution in the UK by Pan Macmillan

Introduction

Asking clever people to tell you their favourite books is always interesting and can be useful. It can prompt you to read a book you've never got round to reading, or to re-read one you'd long forgotten. So when I dreamt up The Week twelve years ago it seemed a good idea to include a best books column – a column that would give readers sometimes surprising ideas of which book to buy next. Instead of wading through newspaper reviews to make our selection, we would ask authors, journalists and anyone else whose views interested us to choose the books they most enjoyed. Out of this simple idea has sprung one of the most popular columns in The Week.

I have often found it helpful. In the early days, for example, Robert Harris chose his favourite thrillers. He included The Day of the Jackal, probably the best thriller written since the war, but also Kalymsky Heights by Lionel Davidson which I'd never heard of but immediately went out and bought – and thoroughly enjoyed. And when both the thriller writer Ken Follett and the former Oxford professor John Bayley chose From Russia with Love as one of their top six, it prompted me to go back to Ian Fleming and be reminded just how stylish and modern his thrillers are.

It's interesting too to note the frequency with which some works occur. You'd expect George Eliot's Middlemarch to be on more than one list, but I've been surprised, over the years, to find that another of my favourites, Anthony Trollope's Framley Parsonage, has been chosen by at least three people, including the journalist and historian Max Hastings. Framley Parsonage is a much slighter novel than Middlemarch, and less well known than, say, Barchester Towers, but it's charming and a joy to read. Not surprisingly, the 19th century novel features a lot, with plenty of Austen and Dickens. John Mortimer chooses Henry James's The Portrait of a Lady, which I'd also choose: "You have to read James regularly to convince yourself that writing novels is a worthwhile occupation," he quotes Graham Greene as saying; Roy Hattersley picks Hardy's Far From the Madding Crowd, which has one of literature's most beguiling heroines and, amazingly for Hardy, a happyish ending.

Our contributors to Best Books, of course, have not just chosen novels. As well as From Russia with Love, for example, John Bayley picks the Collected Poems of Philip Larkin, believing Larkin to be one of the finest two poets of the last 50 years (Betjeman being the other). Both Antony Jay and Jon Snow pick Alan Clark's diaries, Jay for their "truth and honesty", Snow for the way they cut through "the humbug that shrouds so much of public life". Memoirs, biographies, children's books, bathtime books, comic novels… all feature in this collection of columns. And while in the early days it wasn't always easy to get all the books that were recommended, some of them being long out of print, this is no longer a problem. Thanks to the joys of the internet, books may be out of print but they're nearly always obtainable – and I hope that within the 160-plus columns collected for these pages you will find some hidden gems.

Jolyon Connell

Editor's Note and Acknowledgements

A compendium portentiously titled 'World's Best Books' will inevitably invoke the ire of readers who disagree with the titles chosen, and I make no apology for what may appear a somewhat eclectic selection. It was, however, based on the sound principle that given the huge variety published in The Week up until February 2006 – a purely pragmatic cut-off date – one should try and reflect the equally varied nature of both the choosers and their choices. This of course included, as Jolyon Connell noted earlier, specialist authors on their specialist subjects, and those who may not primarily be writers but who nonetheless are known for their talents in allied media.

Obviously many of the contributors appearing here have had books published subsequent to those mentioned in their brief introduction, but because of production lead times we would have been hostages to fortune to list them here. Equally obviously, if you're attracted to their work as a consequence of reading their Best Book choices, any good bookshop will provide you with details. The 'Lit Hit Parade' which appends the main body of this book was, however, based on every Best Books column that had ever appeared up until February 2006 and whilst still inviting criticism from certain quarters, nonetheless provides an instructive reflection on literary populism.

Whatever one's views either way, what is undeniable is the stirling effort made by listings editor Charity Crewe in bringing together the hundreds of columnists and their choices over the last ten years, a task requiring both inspiration and much logistical juggling. Without her this book literally wouldn't have been possible, and whilst I'm issuing the plaudits, special thanks are also due to Xandie Nutting for picture research and Nicola Humphreys who performed various vital editorial tasks.

Mark Williams

Monica Ali

The writer Monica Ali chooses her six favourite short story collections.
*Her novel, **Brick Lane**, is published by Doubleday.*

Issue 419: 26th July 2003

For the Relief of Unbearable Urges by Nathan Englander (Faber & Faber) This is a knock-out debut collection. The first story, The Twenty-Seventh Man, set in Stalin's Russia, had me gagging with jealousy (I was trying to write shorts at the time) and I just kept waiting for him to run out of steam. He didn't.

Hateship, Friendship, Courtship, Loveship, Marriage by Alice Munro (Vintage) This must be one of the world's worst titles. Don't be put off. Munro gets as much into a short story as most writers fit into a novel. Yet her writing is capacious rather than dense; the depth comes from her ability to get to the heart of the human condition.

Miguel Street by V.S. Naipaul (Picador) "A stranger could drive through Miguel Street and just say 'Slum!' because he could see no more. But we, who lived there, saw our street as a world, where everybody was quite different from everybody else." Seen through the eyes of a small boy, the neighbour-hood gives life in all its glory, folly, vanity, joy and woe.

Close Range by Annie Proulx (Fourth Estate) These stories are inspired by the Wyoming landscape, which almost takes on the dimensions of another character. Brokeback Mountain is my favourite; a brave, elegiac tale of two cowboys, love and the open range.

Where I'm Calling From by Raymond Carver (Harvill Press) What Carver tells us is that the power of the uninflected English past tense can be huge – if the words are weighted and freighted just right. Therein lies his secret.

Birds of America by Lorrie Moore (Faber & Faber) What I adore about her is the way she calibrates emotion so perfectly. Her story about a starlet's depression and, elsewhere, her exploration of grief in the aftermath of the death of a cat, tune in so finely to the anxieties and indulgences of our times.

Al Alvarez

The poet and critic Al Alvarez chooses his six favourite books.
*His book, **Poker: Bets, Bluffs and Bad Beats,** is published by Bloomsbury.*

Issue 312: 23rd June 2001

King Lear by William Shakespeare (Oxford University Press).
The greatest of Shakespeare's plays and the most desolate. The force of its bleak, pared-down language is unprecedented, even by Shakespeare's standards.

The Interpretation of Dreams by Sigmund Freud (Oxford University Press). This influenced the 20th century more than any other book and transformed our understanding of the slippery, devious way our minds work. I love Freud's intellectual rigour, the dogged way he follows his ideas through in directions he had not expected or intended. The case histories read like short stories by some great, dark, Russian novelist.

John Donne: The Major Works (Oxford University Press). I fell in love with what Thomas Carew called Donne's "masculine, persuasive force" when I was a schoolboy, and, unlike most youthful infatuations, this one has lasted all my life. I love his aroused, casual tone of voice – alive with feeling yet wholly unsentimental, and sounding like heightened, subtly charged talk – and the way he is always thinking, arguing, even when he is distressed.

The Complete English Poems of George Herbert (Penguin). Herbert had a musician's ear and his poems are technically astonishing. They are lower-keyed than Donne's and more modest, but no less heartbreaking.

Waiting for Godot by Samuel Beckett (Faber). The King Lear of our time. Beckett's vision is equally bleak and his language equally bare, but his particular genius was to make his despair funny without in any way making it less desperate.

The Poems of Zbigniew Herbert (Out of print). Even in translation, this Polish poet is, for me, the greatest of all my contemporaries: a fierce moralist, ironic, clear-eyed and supremely intelligent. No one has written more subtly about what it was like to write under a totalitarian system and remain independent.

Jake Arnott

*Jake Arnott, author of cult books on real-life criminals, chooses his six favourite crime memoirs. His book, **He Kills Coppers,** is published by Sceptre.*

Issue 346: 23rd February 2002

The Autobiography of a Thief by Bruce Reynolds. (Virgin Books). Elegantly written, the mastermind of the Great Train Robbery conveys the glamour and excitement of his exploits but also the cock-ups, the downside of being on the run, the dull horror of imprisonment and institutionalisation.

Walking Away by Hugh Collins (Canongate). The second part of Hugh Collins's autobiography, an ex-lifer coping after 16 years in prison. Always candid, painfully raw and moving, and at times hilariously funny, Collins is a great writer with a wonderfully immediate style which I am glad to say he has now also turned to fiction.

Gentleman Thief by Peter Scott (HarperCollins). As with his modus operandi, so with his prose style Scott has a great sense of panache. The legendary cat burglar writes in the third person, a device which lends a cool detachment to his arch tale of highlife and lowlife.

The Krays' Lieutenant by Albert Donoghue (Pan). Written with Martin Short, a penetrating account by one of the firm who eventually went QE against the brothers. Full of dark humour – "We even called the twins 'Gert' and 'Daisy', but only behind their backs, because every day they resembled a well-known pair of women comedians more and more."

Product of the System by Mark Leech (Gollancz). Leech's story, of how he survived various penal institutions to become an articulate spokesman on prison reform, is outstanding in its honesty and insight. A tribute to the tenacity of the human spirit.

Junkie by William S. Burroughs (Penguin). Originally published as a true-crime memoir in 1953, this remains one of the author's best works. Publishers' note back then: "There has never been a criminal confession better calculated to discourage imitation by thrill-hungry teenagers." And how right they were.

Jane Asher

*Jane Asher, actress and celebrity cake-maker, has also written several popular novels including **The Longing**. Here she chooses six of her favourite books.*

Issue 141: 21st February 1998

The White Hotel by D.M. Thomas (Penguin). A powerful narrative of the Holocaust recounted by a young woman to her analyst, Sigmund Freud. At first bit read like pretentious pseudo poetry, but by the end it hit me for six.

The Black Prince by Iris Murdoch (Penguin). This book contains one of the wittiest and most striking descriptions of falling in love in the English language. Bradley Pearson is an elderly author suffering from writer's block. Surrounded by predatory friends and relations, he attempts to escape.

Anna Karenina by Tolstoy (Oxford University Press). This story of an aristocratic woman who brings ruin on herself is rich in incident, powerful in characterisation and expresses Tolstoy's own moral vision. I was struck by the immense subtlety of the dissection of love and loyalty.

Les Misérables by Victor Hugo (Penguin). Set in Paris after the French Revolution, Hugo recreates events through the lives and experiences of a handful of brilliantly drawn characters. I defy anyone not to cry.

The Mayor of Casterbridge by Thomas Hardy (Penguin). Almost any Hardy could have qualified, but this particular one has the best qualities of all his novels rolled into one.

Perfume by Patrick Suskind (Penguin). An unusual tale about an outcast born with superhuman olfactory powers, which he uses for evil ends. Here, the written word really comes into it own, communicating the horror and emotion of this story in a devastating way.

Jane Austen

*Pride and Prejudice is one of the nation's favourite novels, but what did Jane Austen read herself? Josephine Ross, author of **Jane Austen, A Companion**, lists six of the Regency writer's own best-loved books.*

Issue 408: 10th May 2003

Tales in Verse by George Crabbe (Out of print). Crabbe's lyrical tales are among Fanny Price's treasured books in Mansfield Park. Austen so revered the poet that, though they'd never met, she would often say, "if she ever married at all, she could fancy being Mrs Crabbe".

Sir Charles Grandison by Samuel Richardson (Out of print). Verbose and dated as it may seem today, Richardson's classic novel-in-letters, detailing the trials (and attempted rape) of a virtuous young society woman, was probably Austen's all-time favourite book. In her youth she adapted the seven-volume novel into a five-act play for her family's entertainment.

Waverley by Walter Scott (Penguin). "Scott has no business to write novels, especially good ones… He has fame and profit enough as a poet," protested Austen in 1814. She added, "I do not mean to like Waverley if I can help it, but I fear I must."

The Mysteries of Udolpho by Ann Radcliffe (Penguin). Bristling with secret passages, ghastly apparitions, a locked chest and a missing wife, Mrs Radcliffe's bestseller was among the first, and best, of the "horrid novels" so fondly burlesqued by Austen in Northanger Abbey. "Do not you think Udolpho the nicest book in the world?" enquires Northanger's ingenue heroine.

Essay on the Military Policy and Institutions of the British Empire by C.W. Pasley (Out of print). Captain Pasley's scathing critique of Britain's conduct in the Peninsular War was a book that the patriotic Austen came greatly to admire. "He does write with such extraordinary force and spirit!" she commented.

Life of Samuel Johnson by James Boswell (Penguin). According to her brother Henry, "Johnson in prose" greatly influenced Jane's own style. A devotee of the great essayist and lexico-grapher whom she called "my dear Dr Johnson", she often quoted from Boswell's famous life of him in her letters.

Lynn Barber

Lynn Barber, author, journalist and chief interviewer for The Observer, chooses her six favourite books.

Issue 306: 12th May 2001

Father and Son by Edmund Gosse (Penguin). This is a surprisingly "modern" confessional memoir, though published in 1890. Philip Gosse, the father, was a Plymouth Brother and distinguished naturalist (his book A Naturalist's Sojourn in Jamaica is well worth reading) whose world collapsed with the advent of Darwinism. Edmund Gosse, the son, records his downfall with a cool, unfilial eye.

Scoop by Evelyn Waugh (Penguin). Where would we journalists be without "Up to a point, Lord Copper"? In truth, the novel falls off quite badly once it moves to Abyssinia, but the first section, when Boot is summoned to Fleet Street, is pure joy.

Diaries by Alan Clark (Weidenfeld & Nicolson). The first volume of these superb journals is better than the second, but I'm happy for any excuse to dip into either. I find the rhythm of Clark's prose and the sweep of his mood changes as exhilarating as champagne. Also he makes me laugh on almost every single page.

U and I by Nicholson Baker (Granta). Baker, when young, was obsessed with John Updike and this is a wonderfully funny account of his nerdy pursuit of his hero. But it is also about his passion for literature – his relationship with Updike is much like Nick Hornby's with Arsenal – and is oddly moving.

Sir Vidia's Shadow by Paul Theroux (Penguin). Again, an account of obsession and again, like U and I, written by an unreliable narrator who becomes increasingly unhinged as the story goes on. This makes it almost like a whodunnit, as you try to work out whetherV.S. Naipaul or Theroux is the one behaving badly.

The Sun Also Rises by Ernest Hemingway (Vintage). I love all Hemingway's writing, even the really embarrassing things like Across the River and Into the Trees, but this short novel is probably the least flawed.

Rosemary Bailey

*Rosemary Bailey, author of **Life in a Postcard and Scarlet Ribbons: A Priest with Aids**, chooses her six favourite books about France. Her novel, **The Man who Married a Mountain**, is published by Bantam Press*

Issue 507: 16 April 2005

A Lady's Walks in the South of France in 1863 by Mary Eyre (out of print). Mary Eyre is a grumpy, middle-aged, impoverished but doughty traveller, climbing mountains, singing, botanising, and criticising the slovenly peasants. Her female perspective gives a more authentic sense of the period and place than many male adventurers.

Perfume from Provence by Lady Fortescue (Transworld). The original ex-pats in Provence. In the Thirties, Winifred and her monocled Monsieur restore a house in the mountains, join in the olive harvest and recount hilarious tales of Provencal peasants. It all sounds so familiar.

On the Brink: The Trouble with France by Jonathan Fenby (Time Warner). A refreshing view of France by the former editor of The Observer. Fenby combines a deep love of the country with clear-eyed analysis of its faults and entertaining insider knowledge of its appealing foibles.

Suite Française by Irène Némirovsky. (Published in French by Denoel, translation by Chatto & Windus). A novel about the fall of France, written by a Jewish writer who died in Auschwitz. It's an incredibly moving description of the flight from Paris, with every level of French society exposed at its most venal and vulnerable.

Footsteps: Adventures of a Romantic Biographer by Richard Holmes (HarperCollins). A brilliant combination of travel and biography. Robert Louis Stevenson in the Cevennes, Wordsworth and Mary Wollstonecraft in Paris, brought to life as Holmes immerses himself in the history and atmosphere of each place.

The Foul and the Fragrant: Odour and the French Social Imagination by Alain Corbin. (Pan Macmillan). An enthralling account of the smells and perfumes of France, from the alluring power of body odour to the effect of smell on the literary imagination.

15

Joan Bakewell

Joan Bakewell, the radio and television broadcaster who wrote and presented My Generation and Taboo, chooses her six favourite books.

Issue 367: 20th July 2002

Time will Darken It by William Maxwell (Harvill Press). Maxwell was an editor on The New Yorker for many years and admired by John Updike, among others. I love the beauty of his writing and the fine way he depicts the nuances of relationships in early 20th century middle-America. The plot unfolds from within an unsatisfactory marriage; none of the characters are heroic, simply flawed human beings destined to make a mess of their lives.

The Times Atlas of the World (Times Books). I love maps. They're a different way of reading the world. It's sometimes good to get away from words and cruise the contours of our planet.

An Intimate History of Humanity by Theodore Zeldin (Minerva). This is a totally original way of looking at how we live our lives and what matters to us – family, work, etc. The title is almost forbidding, but the book is rich with people's stories, insights from the byways of history and ideas for how we should live.

Karl Marx by Francis Wheen (Fourth Estate). How can the biography of such an implacably serious man be so thoroughly entertaining? Probably because it is fuelled by the intelligence and humour of its author. This account brings Marx and his times vividly to life and laughter.

One Hundred Years of Solitude by Gabriel Garcia Marquez (Penguin). This made a startling impact when it was first published, more or less inventing magical realism at a stroke. I found it thrilling, so full of imagination, surprises and family angst.

The Leopard by Giuseppe di Lampedusa (Harvill Press). I like books on a grand scale. This is the story of a Sicilian aristocrat coming to terms with the forces of change in 19th century Italy. It is epic and personal at the same time, and one of the rare times when the film (Burt Lancaster's greatest role) matched up to the text.

Raffaella Barker

*The author Raffaella Barker chooses six books with fabulous heroines. Her novel, **Summertime**, is published by Review.*

Issue 303: 21st April 2001

Cowboys Are My Weakness by Pam Houston (Virago). Short stories about daredevil women who fall in love with hunters who ride the white water and hang out in mountain outposts of America's wild country. Twanging country and western music and fur rugs on the floor are the backdrop to broken hearts and cherished dreams. Every girl is a fighter if not a winner.

Vanity Fair by William Thackeray (Oxford University Press). Becky Sharpe is resilient, resourceful and rapacious; her rise and fall are colourful, moving, and sometimes very funny. Set in the Regency, one of my favourite periods of history, and a perfect moment to depict social folly.

The Travelling Hornplayer by Barbara Trapido (Penguin). Beautiful red-haired Stella is her parents' longed-for only daughter, muse to a brilliant artist and then a stricken wife with a tragic secret. Hugely clever, funny and moving, Stella's story entwines with others just as fascinating to create a beautifully balanced and poignant full picture.

My Friend Flicka by Mary O'Hara (Egmont). Ken, a boy growing up on a ranch in Wyoming, is given a colt of his own. He chooses Flicka because she is beautiful and wild. His parents are worried, he goes through hell to break her in, and in doing so creates a legend and grows up himself.

No Name by Wilkie Collins (Penguin). Mercurial, unscrupulous Magdalen is a modern heroine in a 19th century novel about illegitimacy, disinheritance and a fall from social grace. Gripping narrative and unforgettable imagery.

The Constant Nymph by Margaret Kennedy (Virago). Teresa, daughter of a bohemian composer, falls in love at the age of 14 with another gifted composer. Her life in the ramshackle circus of her precocious siblings and father's sluttish mistresses has left her "unbalanced, untaught and fatally warm-hearted". She is sent away to school, but remains constant, haunting and deliciously innocent.

17

Julian Barnes

The author Julian Barnes chooses six of his favourite 20th century American short-story writers. His book, **Love, etc.** is published by Jonathan Cape.

Photo: Ellen Warner

Issue 276: 7th October 2000

Edith Wharton. Mistakenly, her short stories have not enjoyed the revival that her novels have; here there is more ghostliness, and more overt comedy. **The Reckoning and Other Stories** (Phoenix), which contains Roman Fever, can be safely recommended.

Ernest Hemingway. His literary virtues of economy, wryness and disjunction work better in this form than in the full-length novel. The stories also confirm that his great theme is not heroism but cowardice. **Complete Short Stories** (Simon Schuster).

Barry Hannah. Barely published over here, Hannah is a dazzling, lyrical and scary depicter of the American South, with a perfect ear for the redneck cadence. Get his debut collection, **Airships** (Grove & Atlantic).

John Cheever. Cheever's chaotic and tormented life has been allowed to overshadow his controlled and stylish work. **The Collected Stories** (Vintage) are his masterpiece: suburban discontent raised by a transcendent ache and a shimmer of the surreal.

Lorrie Moore. The best American short-story writer under 50. **Birds of America** (Faber & Faber), her latest collection, shows her in full plumage and vertiginous flight, able to range from the comedy of female yearning to the tragedy of infant cancer.

John Bayley

*John Bayley is a former professor of English at Oxford. He was married to the novelist Iris Murdoch. His memoir of their life together, **Iris**, is published by Duckworth. Here he selects six books which never fail to cheer him up.*

Issue 164: 1st August 1998

A Glass of Blessings by Barbara Pym (Pan). The most subtle and funny of all the Pym novels, with echoes of Jane Austen's Emma. Both cosy and disturbing, showing how incomplete life always is, and how it's best to accept the fact.

From Russia with Love by Ian Fleming (Hodder & Stoughton). An absurdly memorable thriller. James Bond has a strange gift of frightening and comforting at the same time, rather like a male version of Barbara Pym.

News from Tartary – A Journey from Peking to Kashmir by Peter Fleming (Abacus). A wonderful travel book by Ian's older brother. Day-by-day account of crossing Mongolia in 1934, with a tent and a Swiss girl with whom he has a mutually happy absence of sexual relations.

The Last Grain Race by Eric Newby (Picador). Before the mast on a wind jammer to Australia in 1938. Splendidly humorous detail about crew, food and ship.

A Ship of the Line by C.S. Forester (Penguin). The best of the Hornblower series. I briefly deserted Forester for the now all-too-fashionable Patrick O'Brian series, but one always comes back to Hornblower in the end.

Collected Poems of Philip Larkin (Faber). With John Betjeman, the finest English poet of the last 50 years. Between them they put all the recent Irish poets in the shade, or rather in their shadow.

19

Sister Wendy Beckett

Sister Wendy Beckett, writer and television presenter, selects her six favourite books on sculpture. Her books include **Max Beckmann and the Self** *and, for children,* **The Duke and the Peasant**, *both published by Prestel.*

Issue 115: 5th July 1997

The Materials of Sculpture (Yale) by Nicholas Penny. No book gives a better awareness of what sculpture actually is, a confrontation with a three-dimensional reality that invades our human space. From malleable clay to obdurate porphyry, Penny shows how matter becomes receptive of form.

Understanding Greek Sculpture: Ancient Meanings, Modern Readings (Thames & Hudson) by Nigel Spivey. This book is an elegant example of the contemporary approach to art, as emphasised in the sub-title. All art, however awesome, has arisen out of a real world and with a real purpose, and Spivey helps us understand this.

In Pursuit of the Absolute: The George Ortiz Collection (Royal Academy). Every ancient civilisation has found sculptural expression. Ortix has collected, and here lovingly discusses, small masterpieces from all over the ancient world.

The Limewood Sculptors of Renaissance Germany (Yale) by Michael Baxendall. Here is scholarship made genuinely exciting, as Baxendall involves us in the tactile glories of the carved figure. This art can be overwhelmingly in the intensity of its exuberance and equally in its almost fanatic control.

An Introduction to Italian Sculpture in three volumes: Gothic, Renaissance and Baroque (Phaidon) by John Pope-Hennessy. Sarcastically referred to as "the Pope", Pope-Hennessy is not literally infallible, but his majestic style can make him seem so. This is an impressively exhaustive survey, never exhausting, of the most prolonged period of creative genius in European history. Superb illustrations too.

Sybille Bedford

*The novelist and biographer Sybille Bedford chooses her six favourite books. Four of her novels, including **A Favourite of the Gods**, have been reissued as Penguin 20th Century Classics.*

Photo: Luciana Arrighi

Issue 207: 5th June 1999

The Decline and Fall of the Roman Empire by Edward Gibbon (Penguin, 3 Vols). The glorious rumble of Gibbon's prose – the clarity, the subtlety, the wit, the sweep of the vast narrative towards the inevitable – this staggering product of a single human mind is a potent link for me with that centre of our Western inheritance: Rome.

Hot Money by Dick Francis (Pan). Odd man out? Certainly a supreme craftsman. Note the economy of his expositions, the skill and drive of his dialogue. I read him also for his joy in the natural world – the morning gallops, the heat of the race. I chose Hot Money for his fascinating insights into nearly two dozen characters.

Un Coeur Simple by Gustave Flaubert (lead story of Trois Contes, Penguin). Here the master is perhaps at his most perfect. When an artist of that order has expended his integrity and labour word on word, something beyond those words comes into being; and here it is, the tale of a noble-hearted servant in 19th century Normandy that moves us to tears.

Lord Byron: Selected Letters & Journals edited by Lesley Marchand (Pimlico). Byron's letters attract by their invigorating masculinity and the ease and spirit of their style. They invite action, fresh air – a gallop on the Adriatic sands – as well as melancholy, reflection, excess.

The Snows of Kilimanjaro by Ernest Hemingway (Arrow). A 20th century master. No one else in our language has so conveyed the exact quality of physical sensations: of drinking, of food, the rope in the hand. This grim, harsh, frightening and intensely beautiful story is Hemingway at his highest level.

A Handful of Dust by Evelyn Waugh (Penguin). In this most brilliant of despairing novels – the story of crass betrayals – concise lines of dialogue fly as arrows to their mark. Comical and devastating.

Antony Beevor

*Antony Beevor, the author of **Stalingrad** (Viking), selects six of the best books about war.*

Issue 171: 19th September 1998

Homage to Catalonia by George Orwell (Penguin). Orwell's personal account of the Spanish Civil War, where he fought as a volunteer and was badly wounded, is unlike all the others. His book endures because its natural honesty shone out at a time when ideology distorted everything.

Life and Fate by Vasily Grossman (Harvill). This novel, based on the battle of Stalingrad, is often ranked with Doctor Zhivago, but I think it is the greatest Russian work of fiction produced this century. The manuscript was confiscated by the KGB in 1961, but somehow a version was smuggled out to Switzerland.

The Face of Battle by John Keegan (Pimlico). This slim book, first published in 1976, did more to change the face of military history than any number of seminars or unreadable academic tomes. It takes three battles – Agincourt, the Somme and Waterloo – and recreates the experiences and likely feelings of the soldiers at the front.

The Cretan Runner by George Psychoundakis (Penguin). This personal account of the Cretan resistance following the German parachute invasion of the island was written by a shepherd boy who proved to be a natural writer. Beautifully translated by Patrick Leigh Fermor.

War in the Val d'Orcia by Iris Origo (Out of print). Iris Origo is best known for her autobiography, Images and Shadows. This book, based on a diary, recounts the daily struggles of a local community and a group of refugees in southern Tuscany during World War II.

The Savage War of Peace by Alistair Horne (Macmillan). To cover a whole war in a single book is always more difficult than it seems, but when it is a guerrilla war and geographically fragmented, the task is appalling. This account of the Algerian struggle for independence, covering both the political and military aspects, is a model history.

Ronan Bennett

The novelist Ronan Bennett chooses his six favourite books.
*His novel, **Havoc In Its Third Year**, was long-listed for the Mann Booker Prize*
and is published by Bloomsbury.

Issue 476: 4th September 2004

The Chant of Jimmy Blacksmith by Thomas Keneally (out of print). Keneally's recent books have become somewhat fatter than this lean early tale of racism and injustice in the Australian Outback. The prose is sharp but dreamlike, and reminds you just what a good writer Keneally can be. Jimmy Blacksmith's struggle against forces he cannot comprehend is coolly and beautifully rendered.

The Naked and the Dead by Norman Mailer (Flamingo). This novel of the Pacific War is a compelling portrait of men under extreme stress. I remember staying up all night to read it, gripped but almost fearful to turn the next page.

The Human Stain by Philip Roth (Vintage). Roth rages but never rants in this provocative meditation on human weakness. We are imperfect, stained. It is the human condition, and attempts to pretend otherwise lead only to hypocrisy and intolerance. No one does sex and politics like Roth.

Disgrace by J.M. Coetzee (Vintage). Similar themes, but where Roth is wrathful Coetzee turns an icy gaze on sexual hypocrisy and political conformism. I admire his honesty, in both subject and style. He makes no concessions, just goes his own way, without regard to literary fashion or the reader's expectations.

The Sword of Honour Trilogy by Evelyn Waugh (Everyman). Comic and tragic, Waugh's novels of the Second World War are quietly moving. I'm not much of a fan of "officers and gentlemen", but it was hard not to be beguiled by Guy Crouchback's decency and gentleness.

The Redundancy of Courage by Timothy Mo (Paddeless Press). Not one of Mo's better-known novels. He tackles big issues of conscience and loyalty in a story of revolution set in a thinly disguised East Timor. And he does it all with wonderful humour and compassion. Where has this huge talent gone?

Marcus Berkmann

Marcus Berkmann, the author and journalist, chooses his six favourite books about cricket. His book, **Zimmer Men: The Trials and Tribulations of the Ageing Cricketer**, *is published by Little, Brown.*

Issue 523: 6th August 2005

Boycs by Leo McKinstry (out of print). No cricketer deserved a serious, thoughtful biography more than Sir Geoffrey Boycott, and this is it. McKinstry is a fan, but also fair-minded, and a better writer than most cricket biographers. Recently republished as **Geoff Boycott: A Cricketing Hero**, which makes it seem like the whitewash it isn't.

The Art of Captaincy by Mike Brearley (Pan Macmillan). Almost a desert island book for me. Brearley raised the stakes in cricket writing forever with this clever manual on man-management. I'm no better a captain for reading his book over and over again, but that's my fault, not his.

Dear Merv by Merv Hughes (Allen & Unwin). Owner of the most aggressive moustache in sporting history, Australian fast bowler Merv Hughes is really a big softy. He saved every letter anyone ever sent him, and published them all in this wonderful book. He had already written an autobiography, but this is a better one, in other people's words.

Basil D'Oliveira by Peter Oborne (Time Warner). The D'Oliveira Affair was one of the most shameful episodes in cricket history, and this is the definitive account, told with authority and passion, which is a tricky balancing act in itself. A work of scholarship, subtlety and moral strength.

A Season In Sinji by J.L. Carr (Quince Tree Press). J.L. Carr was a Kettering-based headmaster, novelist and publisher of pamphlets, including his Dictionary Of Extra-Ordinary Cricketers. But Sinji is the best cricketing novel I have read: set in west Africa during the Second World War, this story of rivalry and exile is funny, wise, strange and sad.

Wisden Cricketers' Almanack, edited by Matthew Engel (John Wisden & Co). Either the current one, which I haven't finished yet, or the next one, which they haven't started yet. Hard to imagine what life would be without it.

Steven Berkoff

Actor and director Steven Berkoff here chooses his six favourite books.

Issue 137: 24th January 1998

The Last of the Just by Andre Scharzbart (Random House, out of print). A fascinating novel on an epic scale which traces the myth of the Jewish "36 Just Men" who are chosen to take on the suffering of the world. Once read, never forgotten.

Against Nature by Joris Huysmans (Penguin). One of those "can't put it down" seminal books that could only be written by a Frenchman. It catalogues the degrees of stimulation possible for the roués who are past the stage of satiation. A phantasmagoria of colours, smell and taste.

The Portrait of Dorian Grey by Oscar Wilde (Penguin). Atmospheric, rich in detail and finely wrought. A greatly moral book, as Wilde's own kindness shines through, but mistaken as an immoral book because it makes decadence attractive, which is precisely the point...

Last Exit to Brooklyn by Herbert Selby Junior (HarperCollins). Down in the sewers of life, in the underbelly where filth and grime are the crossroads of your street, exists the most powerful poetry of the soul to come out of American literature for 50 years. Harrowing, painful and lyrical.

The Magic Barrel by Bernard Malumud (Chatto & Windus, out of print). A collection of short stories so pithy and so moving that they leave you wiser, saddened and amazed by the incredible imagination of this gentle and wistful writer.

Hell by Henri Barbusse (Turtle Point). A hell hound of a book. The grim, acrid reality of a Paris in the time of cold water rooms, Bohemia, sad cafés and sexual obsession.

Maeve Binchy

*Maeve Binchy, the popular Irish novelist, chooses six of her favourite self-help books. Her bestseller, **Tara Road**, is published in paperback by Orion.*

Issue 204: 15th May 1999

The Complete Idiot's Guide to Managing Your Time by Jeff Davidson (Simon and Schuster). This is a book for workaholics, full of advice about how to leave work on time at least one day a week. Who are these guys? You will be greatly reassured that whatever your lifestyle, it's better than that of those who have to be enticed out of their offices.

Notes and Queries edited by Joseph Harker (Fourth Estate). The latest in the series of anthologies of quirky questions sent to The Guardian and answered by even quirkier readers. Questions like: Where was the first banana republic? Things you always wanted to know.

The Silva Mind Control Method by Jose Silva (Simon and Schuster). This is a wonderful book telling you that you can get everything you want in life if you just visualise the way you want to be – rich, confident, thin... whatever it is that turns you on. Of course it doesn't really work, but it drives you wild with excitement reading it.

Dear Mary: Social Dilemmas Resolved by Mary Killen (Constable). I hate most etiquette books with a passion but I love this one. The author seems to understand that it is all barking mad and sends everything up so wildly that it will surely be a great comfort to almost everyone.

The Easy Way to Tree Recognition by John Kilbracken (Kingfisher Books). I just love this book and keep a copy always in my handbag. Even for horticulturally challenged people like myself it has a foolproof system. I'd know a Lombardy Poplar from a Black Poplar at a great distance.

When You Eat at the Refrigerator Pull up a Chair by Geneen Roth (Hyperion). A triumphant self-help book telling you that if you are going to graze at the fridge, do it properly. Sit down in comfort and better still invite other people in to sit with you. It's a satisfying book proving that we are all greedy and full of self-delusion. You'll love it.

Christopher Booker

Christopher Booker, the journalist and author, chooses six books that he would be "pleased to introduce to a reader who didn't know them".
*His book, **A Looking Glass Tragedy**, is published by Duckworth.*

Issue 142: 28th February 1998

The Daughter of Time by Josephine Tey (Mandarin). The detective novel as serious history. Scotland Yard inspector-hero investigates the case against the "monstrous child murderer" Richard III, disclosing the true villains as the Tudor propagandists who turned history on its head.

A Portrait of Elmbury by John Moore (Windrush). This beautifully observed first volume in his Brensham Trilogy provides an unforgettable snapshot of everyday life in the English countryside just before the modern world swept it away.

Seeds of Change by Henry Hobhouse (Macmillan). History can never seem the same again after reading this dazzling account of how five plants – cotton, sugar, tea, quinine and the potato – changed the world.

Indian Country by Peter Matthiessen (Out of print). Thought-provoking account of how the "Red Indians" welcomed Europeans to North America and have been betrayed ever since. The battles continue to this day as white greed discovers the Indian's last tribal sanctuaries to be rich in natural resources.

Into the Whirlwind and Within the Whirlwind by Eugenia Ginsberg (Harvill). Reading almost like a great Russian novel, this is a vivid account of what it is like to be snatched from normal life into Stalin's Gulag Archipelago.

The Shakespearian Ethic by John Vyvyan (Out of print). Provides a brilliant analysis of the patterns underlying several of the mature tragedies and comedies. The most illuminating book on Shakespeare I know.

Alain de Botton

The writer Alain de Botton chooses his five favourite books.
*His book, **Status Anxiety**, is published by Penguin.*

Issue 498: 12th February 2005

Human, All Too Human by Friedrich Nietzsche (Penguin). Perhaps Nietzsche's most readable book. The writing is witty and consolingly bleak. Here is a flavour of what's inside: "There will be few who, when they are in want of matter for conversation, do not reveal the more secret affairs of their friends."

Maxims by La Rochefoucauld (Penguin). Behind almost all these maxims lies a challenge to an ordinary, flattering view of ourselves. La Rochefoucauld shows that we're never far from being vain, selfish and petty – and this is never more true when we trust in our own goodness. We may believe we're concerned about the worries of our friends, but "we all have strength enough to endure the troubles of others" – as he so aptly puts it.

Democracy in America by Alexis de Tocqueville (Penguin). One of the few philosophical travelogues. De Tocqueville travelled to the US in the early 19th century to look into what happens to values in a democratic, mercantile age. The answer is that they can become depressingly commercial.

Art and Illusion by Ernst Gombrich (Phaidon). Gombrich's book is an attempt to write a psychology and philosophy of seeing, as it applies to our responses to the visual arts. It's one of the most thrilling books on art ever to have been written, largely because of the ingenious way in which Gombrich ties together high and low culture, comparing the way we read everything from Constable to a Tube poster.

The Temptation to Exist by E.M. Cioran (University of Chicago Press). Many have complained that philosophy in the 20th century lost the humanity and poetry it once possessed. The work of the Romanian-French philosopher is a triumphant exception to the depressing norm. He wrote beautifully, in short, finely crafted sentences. He is a hero in France, but his books are hardly read over here.

William Boyd

*William Boyd, the novelist and screenwriter, chooses six of the best contemporary collections of essays. His book, **Bamboo: Non-Fiction 1978-2004**, is published by Hamish Hamilton.*

Issue 544: 7th January 2006

More Matter by John Updike (Hamish Hamilton). The prodigious intellect of John Updike is both tireless and eclectic. This is the fourth massive volume of his collected journalism and his output is, frankly, staggering. So is the quality: well into his seventies, Updike proves that energy and insight need never falter.

In Defence of T.S. Eliot by Craig Raine (Picador). Shrewd, scholarly, controversial, Raine's criticism is challenging and exhilarating. The sheer forensic power of his close-reading is daunting and the fearlessness of his views are incredibly stimulating. No judicious equivocation here: just tough, clever argument.

The War Against Cliché by Martin Amis (Vintage). The title says it all: lazy writing beware. Martin Amis has been writing criticism alongside his novels since the early Seventies. Brilliantly stylish (and coolly ferocious when required) his essays show the same bravura and aplomb as his fiction.

Anglo-English Attitudes by Geoff Dyer (Abacus). Dyer's idiosyncratic take on books, photography, travel, music and other enthusiasms is hugely beguiling. No one else makes self-deprecation so tellingly persuasive. But Dyer is the smartest and most selective of commentators: never has nonchalance been mobilised so cunningly and effectively.

Strong Opinions by Vladimir Nabokov (Random House). These are in fact collected interviews but because Nabokov always wrote his answers to interviewers' questions they read like his usual unique prose. Wonderfully, bracingly opinionated.

Collected Essays by Cyril Connolly (Out of print). The great hedonist's wistful, melancholy take on life and literature. Passion for art, enthusiasm for the finer pleasure the world has to offer, clear-eyed autobiography, some on-the-nail parodies plus Connolly's particular blend of amour-propre and self-loathing – the tone of voice is marvellously seductive.

Gyles Brandreth

*Writer and broadcaster Gyles Brandreth chooses his six favourite books. He has published his diaries of his time as an MP, **Breaking the Code**, and a biography of Sir John Gielgud.*

Issue 285: 9th December 2000

The Diary of Samuel Pepys, edited by Robert Latham (HarperCollins). I keep a diary of my own and, most nights, dip into somebody else's as well. I have just finished the diaries of film-maker and Aids victim Derek Jarman and am moving on now to those of playwright Peter Nichols. But you can't beat Pepys: human, humane, unguarded – the first and still the best.

Orley Farm by Anthony Trollope (Oxford University Press). Thackeray's Vanity Fair is my favourite single novel, but Trollope is my favourite author. He never lets you down and Orley Farm has got the lot: laughter, tears, high drama, sweet romance and sharp courtroom scenes.

Twelfth Night by William Shakespeare (Penguin). In my mind I live in Shakespeare's Illyria. I like to read plays and I cast them as I go. I am currently working on Twelfth Night with Blair as Malvolio, the Queen as Olivia, John Prescott as Toby Belch, Mo Mowlam as Maria, and Chris Smith as Andrew Aguecheek.

Winnie-the-Pooh by A.A. Milne (Methuen). For comfort reading I still turn to Arthur Conan Doyle, Frank Richards (the creator of Billy Bunter and the most prolific writer of the 20th century) and A.A. Milne. My proudest boast is that I knew the real Christopher Robin – I shook the hand that held the paw of Winnie-the-Pooh.

The Old Wives' Tale by Arnold Bennett (Penguin). Arguably the best novel written by an Englishman in the past 100 years. If you've not yet read it, get it now.

At Mrs Lippincote's by Elizabeth Taylor (Little, Brown). The first of 11 impeccable novels by Taylor, not the actress, but the Jane Austen of our time. Taylor (1912-75) gives us postwar Middle England: ironic, frequently heartbreaking, always beautifully observed.

Celia Brayfield

*Novelist Celia Brayfield chooses her favourite books about country life. Her town-vs-country comedy, **Wild Weekend**, is published by Time Warner.*

Issue 469: 17th July 2004

Mrs Fytton's Country Life by Mavis Cheek (Faber & Faber). With crisp observation added to the author's signature cynicism about the ways of men and teenagers, this comedy about a menopausal downshifter taking control of her life gently dismembers every modern fantasy of country living.

A Country Life by Roy Strong (Bantam). A collection of Roy Strong's columns in Country Life, illustrated by his late wife, Julia Trevelyan Oman. I could wish that he were less fond of the word "effulgent", but nobody can evoke the joy of the first aconite, the rapturous scent of honeysuckle or the antics of a fat cat with more elegance.

Under The Greenwood Tree by Thomas Hardy (Penguin). A sun-dappled pastoral romance, in which our hero wins the heart of the village schoolteacher and sees off the pretentious new vicar. Hardy crystallised the mythology of Victorian village life in this, his second novel and one of his own favourite works.

Akenfield: Portrait of an English Village by Ronald Blythe (Penguin). This history of a Suffolk community mixes elegiac memories with unsentimental accounts of social divisions. It shows how the decline of farming and impact of war added the weight of social realism to the rural romanticism of the Sixties.

Lark Rise to Candleford by Flora Thompson (Penguin). Artless and delightful, an auto-biographical trilogy about growing up in the Oxfordshire countryside. The author, a builder's daughter who left school at 14, observes both people and nature with loving eyes.

Cold Comfort Farm by Stella Gibbons (Penguin). Still screamingly funny after more than 70 years. The author intended to satirise the earnest primitivism of D.H. Lawrence and acolytes, but her adventures of an orphaned It-girl visiting the primitive Starkadder clan and their farcical livestock endures as a classic in its own right.

Richard Briers

The actor Richard Briers chooses his six favourite books.

Issue 338: 22nd December 2001

The Wind in the Willows by Kenneth Grahame (Penguin). Again, I first read this when I was ten and was instantly captivated. Not only is Grahame a brilliant storyteller, he creates a host of extraordinary characters – all of whom I felt I've met in their human equivalents. To this day I find his beautifully crafted prose quite hypnotic. I played Ratty in Alan Bennett's adaptation for the Royal National Theatre some years ago – a happy memory.

The Inimitable Jeeves by P.G. Wodehouse (Penguin). I played Bertie Wooster to Michael Horderns' Jeeves on Radio 4 and was later transferred to BBC audio books. Michael was the definitive Jeeves and I loved playing Bertie.

Treasure Island by Robert Louis Stevenson (Penguin). I first read Treasure Island when I was ten, and it, more than any other book, made me realise how thrilling reading could be. Jim Hawkins was about my age when he outwits Long John Silver and finds the treasure – excellent fodder for the imagination of impressionable young boys.

Henry Irving: An Actor and his World by Laurence Irving (out of print). The first man to make Shylock sympathetic and the first actor to be knighted. I read this wonderful biography of the eminent Victorian when I was doing my National Service and it spurred me into becoming an actor.

The Complete Sherlock Holmes by Sir Arthur Conan Doyle (Penguin). I never tire of rereading the adventures of Sherlock Holmes and Dr Watson. Holmes first appears in A Study in Scarlet and continues making his brilliant deductions through this gripping collection.

Garrick by Ian McIntyre (Penguin). Another thesp, David Garrick emerges from this biography as one of the most glamorous figures of 18th century England. It is packed with detail and masses of fascinating people; Garrick was a superb actor and a great networker.

Asa Briggs

Asa Briggs, historian of Victorian England, selects six books which influenced him as an undergraduate at Cambridge and which he still re-reads.

Issue 108: 28th June 1997

Portrait of an Age by G.M. Young (Oxford University Press, out of print). A portrait, not a treatise, it retains its freshness. It remains the most stimulating approach to the Victorian age, which I was never formally taught but which has fascinated me since.

Rural Rides by William Cobbett (Penguin). No man wrote more directly and more forcefully. His pictures of landscapes, most of which have changed dramatically, are unforgettable. I am pulled by his radicalism, but do not share most of his prejudices. He wanted "to make my country worth living in".

England and the English by Lord Lytton (Greg Internat). Long before the study of "Englishness" became fashionable, the brilliant author of The Last Days of Pompeii, not a favourite of mine, made me think. Still very much to the point.

Moral Man and Immoral Society by Reinhold Niebuhr (Scribners). This penetrating book, published one year before Hitler came to power, saved me from utopianism without turning me into a cynic. Described as "filled with learning, lightened by brilliance, and inspired by insight".

Scoop by Evelyn Waugh (Penguin). I learned more about immoral men and women from Waugh, our greatest 20th-century writer, than from any other contemporary novelist, and something different, too, about immoral society.

The Decline of the West by Oswold Spengler (Out of print). This ponderous but beguiling book brings together, not always convincingly, so many complex themes in Europe's history and culture that I found it difficult to put down.

Raymond Briggs

*Raymond Briggs, author of The Snowman (Puffin), chooses his six favourite books. His **UG, Boy Genius of the Stone Age** and **Search for Soft Trousers** are published by Arrow.*

Issue 324: 15th September 2001

Rotten To The Core by Francis Selwyn (Out of print).
The biography of George Neville Heath, the murderer hanged in 1946. Fascinating to read how someone completely insane could be well-liked and successful after his disgrace. Shows how good looks, charm and officer-class manners could let someone get away with murder – almost.

Giles' Cartoons (Out of print).
The first ever Giles book and the best. Superb vast backgrounds of war townscapes and skies. Brilliantly funny about Americans and the absurdities of Nazism. Given to me by my Auntie Bertha when I was 12. Cost three and six pence. Now worth at least £250.

Smallcreep's Day by Peter Currell Brown (Out of print)
A marvellous surreal satire on modern industrial life. Should be a film by Terry Gilliam. I sent it to him, but the bugger never replied. One of the most underrated books of the century.

The Adventures of Rupert
(Out of print). An annual I had before the war. It is by Mary Tourtel, Rupert's original creator and by far the best of Rupert artists. Beautiful, simple, quiet, poetic pictures which make magical happenings seem as natural as a cow in a field.

Bomber by Len Deighton (HarperCollins). A minute-by-minute reconstruction of a British bomber raid on Germany, seen from both sides. Ex-bank clerks and school teachers raining tons of high-explosive and fire bombs down on women and children and hospitals.

The British Character by Pont of Punch (Out of print). One of England's greatest cartoonists. Scratch, amateurish drawings which sum up and satirise the period when England was still English; never mind the "British" of the title.

Christopher Brookmyre

*Crime novelist Christopher Brookmyre chooses six books that make him laugh out loud. His book, **All Fun and Games Until Somebody Loses an Eye**, is published by Little, Brown.*

Issue 518: 2nd July 2005

Swing Hammer Swing! by Jeff Torrington (Vintage). A surreal portrait of Sixties Glasgow, related via the keen – if well-bevvied – eyes and coruscating patter of amateur philosopher, father-to-be and diligently dedicated waster Tam Clay. The essence of my home city finely distilled; every dram is a relished drop.

Catch 22 by Joseph Heller (Vintage). Only the most absurd novel could even begin to convey the true insanity of war, and Heller's masterpiece fuses the comic and the tragic to do just this. It renders war a world not of heroes, but of individual survival, where the greatest enemies are those who make us fight.

The Far Corner by Harry Pearson (Time Warner). A one-season tour following football at all levels – from amateur to Premiership – in northeast England, exploring how the sport permeates the community. The funniest book I've read about football. It should be compulsory reading for all glory-hunters who support big teams based miles from where they live.

Pretty In Pink by Jonathan Bernstein (St Martin's Press US). An exhaustive, definitive and well-researched archive of that most critically treasured and culturally invaluable cinematic genre: the Eighties teen movie. Cahiers du Cinema was never like this.

The Thought Gang by Tibor Fischer (Vintage). Depicting the world's least likely but most cerebral crime spree, a series of "philosophical" bank heists pulled off by a fugitive academic and a one-armed, armed robber. Thoroughly tickles the intellectual and scatological funny bones, sometimes simultaneously.

The Law of the Playground by Jonathan Blyth. (Ebury). A compendium of school-days argot, anecdotes and possibly actionable confessions, illustrating the boundlessly inventive cruelty of children. Perhaps the most important human psychology textbook of the new century.

Craig Brown

The humourist Craig Brown chooses his six favourite reference books.
His book, **1966 And All That**, is published by Hodder.

Issue 542: 17th December 2005

Brewer's Rogues, Villains and Eccentrics (Orion). Brilliantly funny encyclopaedia of rum sorts – Jeffrey Archer, Dr Crippen, Doris Stokes – all exquisitely cross-referenced, the creation of the profoundly offbeat satirist William Donaldson, who died this year.

The 20th Century Day by Day (Out of print). Full of photos and written in bouncy journalese, it's easily the best reference book for relating historical events to everything else going on at the time. To take a page at random – August 1984, a man shoots 20 people at a McDonald's in California, Clive Ponting is charged with an offence under the Official Secrets Act and Richard Burton, J.B. Priestley and Truman Capote all die.

British Hit Singles (Guinness World Records). This is the Burke's Peerage of the pop world, listing with an almost mystical pedantry the dates and positions of the vinyl offspring of everyone from the grandest of the grand (Sir Elton, Sir Mick, Sir Paul) all the way down to St Winifred's School Choir's There's No One Quite Like Grandma, number 1 on 22 Nov 1980).

20th Century Words edited by John Ayto (Out of print). Blissfully interesting etymology of words born in the 20th century, ordered by decade, complete with first spotting. Everything from Abominable snowman (1921) to Zit (1966) via Undies (1906) and Slaphead (1990).

The London Encyclopaedia edited by Ben Weinreb and Christopher Hibbert (Pan Macmillan). There are 5,000 entries for London locations – streets, parks, shops – and an index of over 8,000 Londoners: history made mystical through a miracle of compression.

Birds Britannica by Mark Cocker and Richard Mabey (Vintage). Did you know that a swift may fly continuously for three years without touching down and that a kingfisher can catch up to 150 fish a day? This beautiful, lyrical book is as un-anoraky as can be, has about 20 such facts on every page, and never loses its sense of wonder.

Julie Burchill

*Julie Burchill, the journalist and author, chooses her six favourite comic novels. Her book, **Married Alive**, is published by Orion.*

Issue 246: 11th March 2000

Cold Comfort Farm by Stella Gibbons (Penguin). When they're forcing you to read D.H. Lawrence at school, you think the world must be a truly mad place if anyone can read about the "dark flowers of manhood" without cracking up. This book will reassure you that it was Lawrence, and the rest of those writers who confused gardening with sex, who had the wrong end of the stick.

The Country Life by Rachel Cusk (Picador). Beautifully orchestrated miniature with echoes of Cold Comfort Farm. If Miss Cusk wasn't so beautiful, she'd sell a lot more. But people don't like someone having it all so they buy Helen Fielding instead.

Redhill Rococco by Shena Mackay (Vintage). Miss Mackay is Britain's greatest living writer, and this is her funniest book. The allure of mature working-class women to middle-class boys has rarely been better captured as Luke Ribbons attempts to woo sweet-factory worker Pearl Slattery over a long, sultry summer. Mackay is always surprising, which is far more fun than being shocking.

Diary of a Nobody by George Grossmith (Penguin). Grossmith was a journalist by day, an actor by night and a morphine addict by choice. He still found time to write this brilliant book, of which Lord Rosebery said: "I consider a room without a copy of it to be unfurnished."

Good as Gold by Joseph Heller (Black Swan). Deracinated Jews in American academia attempt to suck up to the brain-dead Gentile establishment. There is a hilarious scene in which Gold confides that his test of a friend would be someone who would have hidden him from the Nazis. "I wouldn't have hidden you!" says the Gentile, shocked. "I'm sorry if I gave you that idea!" America the Beautiful with the gloves off.

As Good as it Gets by Simon Nolan (Quartet). Brilliant Brighton novel about friendship, theft and cocaine, audaciously based on the plot of Shallow Grave (one of the characters even remarks on the resemblance!) but much better.

A.S. Byatt

A.S. Byatt, the author and critic, chooses her six favourite biographies.
*Her novel, **The Biographer's Tale**, is published by Chatto & Windus.*

Issue 280: 4th November 2000

Brief Lives by John Aubrey (Penguin). His Brief Lives of eminent 17th century persons is witty, sometimes scurrilous, full of scraps of surprising information and dashingly written. In many ways the beginning of the English biographical obsession, and still a delight to read.

The Quest for Corvo by J.A. Symons (Quartet). This is the biography as detective hunt describing Symons's discovery of clues and shocks in his search for the strange homosexual writer and failed priest, Fr. (Frederick, not Father, a typical deceptive gesture) Rolfe, author of Hadrian the Seventh. This book invented a new narrative form – research as quest.

A Sultry Month by Alethea Hayter (Robin Clark). Describes, in fascinating day-by-day detail, the month of the suicide of the painter B.R. Haydon and the elopement of the Brownings. A pioneer group biography, and a beautifully written and gripping work of art.

The Ladies of Llangollen by Elizabeth Mavor (Penguin). A touching and comic account of the elopement of two Irish noblewomen in 1778, and how they created a perfect rural retirement together in Wales, and became a national example of domestic happiness.

Ludwig Wittgenstein by Ray Monk (Vintage). A perfect example of the right biographer for a complicated person and a distinguished mind. Monk understands both Wittgenstein's thought and its context, and the family and cultural forces that fashioned his puritan perfectionism.

Victor Hugo by Graham Robb (Macmillan). An astounding action-packed life of a French literary and political monument. It's told with dash and panache and is better than most novels for suspense and emotion.

John Carey

*John Carey is Professor of English Literature at Oxford. His choice of the most enjoyable 20th century books appeared in The Sunday Times, and is published as **Pure Pleasure** by Faber. These are his pre-20th century choices.*

Issue 273: 16th September 2000

Troilus and Criseyde by Geoffrey Chaucer (Oxford University Press). This infinitely subtle verse-novel, written well before novels were officially invented, shows that knowledge of the human heart has not advanced one jot since the 14th century.

Northanger Abbey by Jane Austen (Penguin). Not everyone's preference, but of the six great novels this seems to me the champagne, and its touching, witty portrayal of young love is unmatched in fiction. Austen's bugbears, the brash, shallow, pushy Thorpes, are the sort of young people much fêted nowadays.

Paradise Lost by John Milton (Penguin). As sumptuous as a symphony orchestra and as intricate as the score they play from, Milton's epic introduces the first Romantic hero, Satan, and questions the Christian God so acutely that He has never looked the same since.

Great Expectations by Charles Dickens (Penguin). From its first scene on the mist-shrouded marshes, this is Dickens at his most dream-like or nightmarish, thinking himself back into the fearsome world that children inhabit. The heroine, Estella, reflects his love for the young actress Ellen Ternan.

Vanity Fair by William Thackeray (Penguin). The only English novel that, in scope and subject, rivals Tolstoy's War and Peace. Its cynicism and its refusal to glorify war (as even Tolstoy does) are refreshing. Its hero, Dobbin, has true moral sensitivity; a rare thing.

Robert Browning's Selected Poems (Penguin). Browning is the brainiest English poet and he was fascinated by people. He creates a world of passionate human types, all vociferating and cerebrating furiously. By comparison all 20th century poetry is an echo-chamber, inhabited by ghosts.

Justin Cartwright

Justin Cartwright, winner of the Whitbread Novel of the Year award for **Leading the Cheers**, *and author of* **Half in Love**, *chooses his six favourite biographies or autobiographies.*

Issue 294: 17th February 2001

The Long Affair by Conor Cruise O'Brien (Chicago University Press). This book concentrates on Thomas Jefferson's love of France. From his gardens at Monticello to the design of the cupola of the University of Virginia, Jefferson decided French classicism was the shining path. He was also a philosopher in his political life, a fierce rationalist.

Timebends: A Life by Arthur Miller (Methuen). This is not very well written, and has moments of almost sophomoric awkwardness. But it is still a phenomenally interesting book, with a cast of characters from actors to producers to the simple folk among whom Miller grew up. It speaks – sings – of a lost world.

Baden-Powell by Tim Jeal (Out of print). Jeal's assessment of B-P as remarkable, resourceful and a wonderful eccentric, is fair and generally favourable, even if the man himself is more than a little comical.

The Life of My Choice by Wilfred Thesiger (Flamingo). There is something deeply appealing about Thesiger's life. He decided early on the places and people that appealed to him and stuck to his choice. Being a confirmed bachelor loosened his ties to any domestic life, which probably made this easier, but his combination of patrician romanticism and fine visual talent makes this a remarkable book.

Mandela by Anthony Sampson (HarperCollins). Sampson gets right to the root of why Mandela is such a remarkable person: a strong, traditional education, some remarkable teachers and mentors and a cause, to quote the deathless lines, "for which I am prepared to die".

Self-Consciousness by John Updike (Penguin). Although this isn't a full-scale autobiography, it comes pretty close. Updike is the most human of men; he has what is conspicuously lacking in literary figures – a conscientious, thoughtful, diligent approach to his craft and life. I find his observations on the human condition illuminating and uplifting.

Alan Clark

*Alan Clark MP chooses six books which he turns to again and again. His best-selling **Diaries**, were published by Weidenfeld & Nicolson and later dramatised by the BBC.*

Issue 172: 26th September 1998

First, in every sense, comes **The Tale of Peter Rabbit** by Beatrix Potter (Warne). This novel has everything, and no text has ever been accompanied by such observant and delightful illustration.

Next, leave the infantry and learn that it was just as nasty at 20,000 ft. **Eighth Air Force Bomber Stories** (Stephens) was compiled by Russell Zorn, the USAAF photographer assigned to recording crashes. Here are the crews of each aircraft lined up for their official photograph. Their chances of survival were slim – and their expressions show it. Turn the page and there lies the wreckage of yet another B17.

How did we get into this mess? Of all personal records the most absorbing are **The Cadogan Diaries** by Sir Alexander Cadogan (Out of print). Daily account of the efforts of the British governing class to defer the reckoning. Guile, despair, naiveté, elation and melancholy illuminate the mood of this most senior and aristocratic FO official.

Finally, to cheer you up: Evelyn Waugh's **The Great Gilbert Pinfold** (Penguin £6.99). By far the funniest book I have read since I was a schoolboy. The ultimate satire, and whole chunks I can quote from memory.

To no avail. The Upper Classes went under. First they lost too many sons in Flanders; then the Labour government of 1945 broke them up. To appreciate what happened you should read **No Voice From The Hall** by John Harris (John Murray). The mass abandonment of the great houses to dry rot and vandalism is bounteously supported by heart-rending photographs.

Very different is **The Forgotten Soldier** by Guy Sajer (Orion). Badly marketed by its publishers, demand has kept it in and out of print since 1972 on sheer merit. Better than All Quiet on the Western Front.

Jonathan Coe

The writer Jonathan Coe chooses his favourite life stories.
His novel, **The Rotters' Club***, was adapted by the BBC and its sequel,*
The Closed Circle*, is out in paperback.*

Issue 515: 11th June 2005

The Book What I Wrote by Eddie Braben (Hodder & Stoughton). In a sane world, Braben – whose brilliant scripts for Morecambe and Wise brought pleasure to millions in the Seventies – would have streets named after him by now, or at the very least be made Lord Braben of Pwllheli. Still, he seems too happy to care. A joyous book.

Never Apologise by Lindsay Anderson (Plexus). The collected writings of Britain's best postwar filmmaker. Illuminating about his own films and those of Hitchcock, Carol Reed, Michael Powell and others. Required reading for students who believe that British cinema started with Trainspotting.

Rosamond Lehmann: A Life by Selina Hastings (Vintage). An exemplary biography of a writer whose novels seem claustrophobic to some: Lehmann's heroines live inside an emotional hothouse, eternal slaves to their romantic impulses. It sounds as though she lived her own life the same way.

Heartland by Neil Cross (Scribner). Growing up lonely and confused in Scotland, bullied for his Englishness and in the care of a wayward stepfather, Neil Cross somehow pulled through and emerged as a fine writer. This memoir of a fractured childhood is even better than his novels.

Trawl by B.S. Johnson (Out of print). Johnson believed that "telling stories is telling lies", so he gave up writing fiction and in this book – published in 1966 – delved back into his childhood memories. In a way he kick-started the genre of which Neil Cross's book is such a good recent example.

Stuart: A Life Backwards by Alexander Masters (Perennial). A Cambridge academic's story of his own friendship with a homeless, heroin-addicted criminal, which demolishes many of the myths surrounding the so-called "underclass". Already considered a classic.

John Cole

*John Cole, author, journalist and former political editor of the BBC, chooses his six favourite books. His novel, **A Clouded Peace**, is published by Orion.*

Issue 356: 4th May 2002

Tempestuous Journey by Frank Owen (Out of print). This is not the best biography of Lloyd George, but it is an exciting account of the life of Britain's greatest radical statesman, and I read it at an impressionable age. This made me realise that all great men have flaws, but that you must enjoy the heroic bits and live with the imperfections.

Middlemarch by George Eliot (Penguin). This is the great English novel. Dickens is often more entertaining, but Eliot more profound and life-enhancing. She lived up to her own maxim, that one of the purposes of fiction is to make us understand how people feel who are totally different from ourselves.

Mere Christianity by C.S. Lewis (Penguin). The best-known, and possibly the best book by our foremost Christian apologist. Lewis had the common sense to know that the sin in the legend of the Garden of Eden had nothing to do with sex, and everything to do with selfishness. Which is the heart of the matter.

Lucky Jim by Kingsley Amis (Penguin). Jim Dixon's inebriated lecture before a horrified academic audience is the classic comic text, but if I need, for health's sake, to laugh out loud, I am still inclined to turn to the account of his Professor's driving habits and their effect on Dixon.

Therapy by David Lodge (Penguin). Flows easily from the crazy therapies induced by an injured knee, through the supposed philanderings of a tennis professional who turns out to be gay, on to Kierkegaard, and to a pilgrimage to Santiago de Compostella, in pursuit of a child-hood sweetheart. Picaresque, you might say, but funny and moving.

Love in the Time of Cholera by Gabriel Garcia Marquez (Penguin). A powerful story of fruitful or frustrated love, in youth, middle age, and near-senescence, against an exotic background of war, disease and impossible hygiene. Better than Mills & Boon any day.

Joseph Connolly

*Comic novelist and literary biographer Joseph Connolly chooses his favourite novels. His novel, **SOS**, is published by Faber and Faber.*

Issue 360: 1st June 2002

Although I can admire from a distance many Russian, French and American novels (Dostoevsky, Zola, Tom Wolfe), all of my absolute favourites are decidedly English. Just about anything by Charles Dickens, of course, but a true little gem is **A Christmas Carol** (Penguin). Everyone knows the story of Scrooge, though few seem to have actually read it – give yourself a brief but dazzling treat and do so.

George and Weedon Grossmith's **The Diary of a Nobody** (Penguin) is quite timeless, and the forerunner of the modern English comic novel. It was very ahead of its time in its everyday observation, deadpan wit and timing.

Thomas Hardy's **Jude the Obscure** (Penguin) is the novel that has come closest to breaking my heart. Hardy was so hurt and appalled by its critical reception (most found it too inexpressibly painful) that he vowed never again to write another novel, and nor did he.

And so to Kingsley Amis. His first novel, **Lucky Jim** (Penguin), is really his best – and still very funny – but attention should also be given to what is in many ways its sequel, Jake's Thing (out of print), as well as what could be the prequel, the very fine You Can't Do Both (out of print). Together they form the splendid and underrated Jim Dixon trilogy.

P.G. Wodehouse remains the master, of course – any of his ninety-odd novels will do very nicely, thank you – but maybe the most perfect of all the Jeeves and Wooster books is **Joy in the Morning** (Penguin). Sheer bliss.

Critical opinion of **Brideshead Revisited** (Penguin) waxes and wanes. Down the decades, it has variously been described as both Evelyn Waugh's worst and best novel – an embarrassment of riches and religion, or else a tour de force, pure and simple: it certainly works for me.

Shirley Conran

*Shirley Conran, author of **Superwoman** and founder of the Work-Life Balance Trust, chooses the seven best books she has read recently.*

Issue 325: 22nd September 2001

Politics on the Couch: Citizenship and the International Life by Professor Andrew Samuels (Profile Books). Lucid prose, smooth-flowing as a mountain stream. Packed with original and stimulating ideas on economics, nationalism, leadership, fatherhood and other institutions that need examination.

Dr Johnson's London by Liza Picard (Phoenix Press). Gossipy social history; a paper time-machine that transports you back to the 18th century, when wine was considered the best antiseptic, orphans were sold to chimney sweeps for less than the price of a terrier, and out-of-control policemen killed people by mistake – can you believe it?

The State We're In by Will Hutton (Vintage). A humanitarian, sane view of politics and economics by the man who invented the phrase "The Stakeholder Society".

The Great Food Gamble by John Humphrys (Hodder & Stoughton). Humphrys sets out his complicated case with chilling simplicity: that we are eating poison, often in order to enrich protected multinationals.

On the Black Hill by Bruce Chatwin (Random House). As a child during World War II, I was evacuated to the Welsh border country, so I recognise and relive the background of this poignant, multi-faceted novel of Welsh farming twins.

The Undiscovered Chekhov translated by Peter Constantine (Duckworth). These 51 new stories by Anton Chekhov are a bookworm's treasure trove. Many are experimental, most were written in his mid-twenties, all demonstrate the beguiling exuberance of this formidable minimalist.

The Serial by Cyra McFadden (Prion). Newsweek called it "one of the most delicious acts of cultural sabotage since Mark Twain". A comic classic about a year in the life of a Seventies Californian family attempting to keep up with their neighbours. Open it at any page and you will laugh aloud.

Artemis Cooper

*Artemis Cooper, the author and historian, chooses her six favourite books. Her book, **Writing at the Kitchen Table: The Authorised Biography of Elizabeth David**, is published by Viking.*

Issue 258: 3rd June 2000

The World of the Shining Prince by Ivan Morris (Kadansha). A vivid description of court life in 10th century Japan. I read it aged 12, and found a world where money, beauty and love were treated in totally unfamiliar ways.

A Time of Gifts by Patrick Leigh Fermor (Penguin). In 1933, at the age of 18, Fermor began a walk that lasted a year and a half, taking him from the Hook of Holland to Istanbul. In the plains and mountains of middle-Europe, life – whether that of a shepherd, a tavern-keeper or a nobleman – had scarcely changed for centuries. Fermor describes it all with boundless enthusiasm.

Citizens by Simon Schama (Penguin). One of the most exciting books written on the French Revolution. Schama steers you through the assemblies, committees and conventions that unleashed so much blood and bureaucracy, while never loosing sight of the people and ideas that drove the Revolution forward.

The Raj Quartet by Paul Scott (University of Chicago Press). Scott shows how thin the veneer of Anglo-Indian relations during the Raj actually was. This book also contains two brilliantly chilling characters: Ronald Merrick and Mildred Layton.

Behind the Wall: A Journey through China by Colin Thubron (Penguin). This book made me feel I had seen China in a way that no tourist, travelling in an air-conditioned bus, ever could.

The Cairo Trilogy by Naguib Mahfouz (Black Swan). Never was a novelist more like God. Mahfouz understands how the most mundane detail can set someone on a train of thought that leads to the heart of his innermost fears and preoccupations. The trilogy also charts Cairo's transition from an almost medieval city into a modern capital.

Jilly Cooper

*The author Jilly Cooper chooses her five favourite bathtime books. Her novel, **Score!**, is published by Bantam.*

Issue 218: 21st August 1999

The Diary of a Provincial Lady by E.M. Delafield (Virago). One of the funniest, most charming books ever written. In this everyday story of Thirties village life, our gentle heroine battles with pompous vicars, recalcitrant servants, bossy charity committees and a not always appreciative family.

Maxims by Le Rochefoucald (Penguin). This little book of disquiet, penned by a French Duke, was first published in 1665. His reflections on human nature are cynical but unnervingly truthful. For example: "A neighbour's ruin is relished by friends and enemies alike" and "We give nothing so liberally as our advice".

The Field Guide to the Wild Flowers of Great Britain (Readers Digest). One of my nightly pleasures is identifying in this lovely book the flowers I have seen while walking during the day. The drawings are both beautiful and accurate, and the folklore about each plant romantic and poetic.

Music at Night and Other Essays by Aldous Huxley (Out of print). Scour the second-hand bookshops for this superb collection. Huxley carries his massive education so lightly, whether he is describing the dumbing down of intellectuals, the genius of Homer or listening in religious ecstasy to Beethoven. The last essay, in which Huxley advises a budding novelist to learn about human beings by acquiring two feline friends, contains the best writing about cats I have ever read.

Robert Browning: Selected Poetry (Penguin). After Shakespeare, Browning knew more about human nature than any other English poet. Within these pages is a splendid collection of hedonistic bishops, "mistresses with smooth marbly limbs" and spiteful monks. Here is Browning on the cOxford University Press de foudre: "He looked at her as a lover can/She looked at him as one who awakes/The past was a sleep and her life began."

Richard Cork

Art critic and historian Richard Cork chooses his six favourite books.
***Annus Mirabilis?**, a collection of his art criticism, is published by Yale University Press.*

Issue 483: 25rd October 2004

White Noise by Don DeLillo (Picador). The first novel I read by DeLillo, who has become one of my favourite American writers. Comic, tragic, hysterical, sick and confused, this book tracks the life of Jack Gladney, who teaches Advanced Nazism in a small Middle America college.

The Waste Land by T.S. Eliot (Faber). Although it helped define 20th century poetry, I don't see why The Waste Land shouldn't strike just as deep at the beginning of the 21st. Its pessimism, reflecting the aftermath of World War I, still speaks with painful clarity to anyone affected by the anxieties of life today.

Middlemarch by George Eliot (Penguin). Middlemarch enthralled me when I first read it in the Sixties. It is Tolstoyan in depth, even though Eliot's focus on life in a provincial town is far removed from the epic scope of War and Peace. Her exploration of human nature remains unsurpassed.

The Letters of Vincent Van Gogh (Constable & Robinson). The best book of writing on art I have read. I found Van Gogh's attitude an inspiration when struggling with my own apprentice efforts at art criticism. He believed that, if you remember the art you love, you are "never empty of thoughts or truly lonely".

Herzog by Saul Bellow (Penguin). "If I am out of my mind, it's all right with me, thought Moses Herzog." From the very first sentence, Bellow ensures that readers get inside the turbulent, inventive, absurd, perceptive, and untrustworthy brain of his anti-hero. A master of supple prose.

Thorn by Vena Cork (Headline). This debut novel is the best I've read this year. I'm biased, of course: the author is my wife. But it is an outstanding achievement, moving with inexorable force from troubled family life in London to a truly chilling climax.

Bernard Cornwell

The author Bernard Cornwell chooses his six favourite books.
*His novels, **Sharpe's Prey** and **The Gallow's Thief**, are published by Grafton.*

Issue 307: 19th May 2001

The Face of Battle by John Keegan (Pimlico). A seminal work that examines the battles of Agincourt, Waterloo and the Somme from the points of view of the combatants – terrified, confused and elated. It's also the best military history ever written and a huge influence on all of us who describe battles in mere words.

Right Ho, Jeeves by PG Wodehouse (Everyman). I'd recommend any of the Jeeves books, or any of Wodehouse's books. They are impossible to summarise, except to say they are still the funniest books ever written. Except perhaps for Flashman by George MacDonald Fraser. Jeeves meets Flash? Now there's a thought.

Pepys's Diary (HarperCollins). I have the 11-volume set and do not tire of it. Real history, no varnish, and an endless lesson that there is nothing new under the sun. Pepys is a yuppie, and not an attractive one at times, but he redeems himself by his brutal honesty.

Religion and the Decline of Magic by Keith Thomas (Penguin). This is one of those books that changes the way we observe history. It deals with popular apprehensions of the supernatural in the 16th and 17th centuries, but is replete with a wider wisdom.

Wellington at Waterloo by Jac Weller (Greenhill Books). Wellington emerges triumphant from this cold-blooded assessment – one of a trilogy written by Weller, an American engineer obsessed by the Duke.

Wolf Solent by John Cowper Powys (Penguin). I have long been a fan of Powys and especially of his Wessex novels, of which this is one. Powys is little read now, but he is odd, magical, sprawling and intense. Like Thomas Hardy on ecstasy.

Amanda Craig

*Amanda Craig, the novelist and journalist, chooses her six favourite children's books. Her fifth novel, **Love in Idleness**, is published by Time Warner.*

Issue 362: 15th June 2002

The Gruffalo by Julia Donaldson & Axel Schiffer (Macmillan). My favourite picture-book is Where the Wild Things Are, but this comes a close second. A mouse looks for food in the woods, and has to outwit predators by claiming to be meeting his friend the Gruffalo. Then, to its horror, the Gruffalo turns out to be real – and hungry.

A Wizard of Earthsea by Ursula le Guin (Puffin) Long before Harry Potter, le Guin thought of what a school for wizards might be like. The lead character, Ged, is tempted by spells beyond his powers and unleashes a terrible beast. The beauty and precision of this novel's language is extraordinary.

The Chimneys of Green Knowe by Lucy M. Boston (Out of print). All of the Green Knowe novels are outstanding, combining a sense of place (the East Anglian Fens), history and character. Chimneys is about a friendship between a blind girl called Susan and a black slave boy. There are umpteen rubbishy books for children about disability and racism, but this makes me cry and laugh each time.

Journey to the River Sea by Eva Ibbotson (Macmillan) Ibbotson's magical adventures are captivating. In this book, the orphaned Maia travels to the Amazon to live with her evil aunt and uncle. The exotic details of life in Edwardian Brazil are as enthralling as the plot.

His Dark Materials by Philip Pullman (Scholastic Press). Pullman deservedly became the first children's author to win the Whitbread Book of the Year for the third part of this imaginative and gripping inversion of Paradise Lost.

A Necklace of Raindrops by Joan Aiken (Red Fox). Joan Aiken is one of the greatest living children's authors, but most parents only seem to try The Wolves of Willoughby Chase. The sequels, this one in particular, are far better.

Sue Crewe

Sue Crewe, the editor of House and Garden, former editor of Jennifer's Diary and a qualified dairy farmer, chooses her six favourite books.

Issue 269: 19th August 2000

Black Beauty by Anna Sewell (Penguin). The first book I read on my own. Thrilling life story of a horse packed with heroes, villains and tragedy. Despite a happy ending there are some rough passages of human perfidy in the face of equine nobility.

In Patagonia by Bruce Chatwin (Vintage). A traveller's tale of a quest for a strange beast in the southern tip of South America. I read it while visiting Patagonia and it added an extra dimension to the journey. There are descriptions of events that occurred within living memory which stretch credulity, but become less strange in the context of such a remote and beautiful place.

The Royal Horticultural Society A-Z Encyclopaedia of Garden Plants (Dorling Kindersley). Essential for actual gardening and an enjoyable tool for virtual gardening. The tome runs to 1,080 pages, features over 15,000 plants, 6,000 photographs and weighs 4.5 kgs. This one should stay at home and the paperback RHS Good Plant Guide can go on expeditions.

Encyclopaedia of Britain by Bamber Gascoigne (Macmillan). I love reference books and this one is the best browse ever. The 6,000 entries cover historical facts, pop stars, art, scandals, disasters, and everything in between. Charmingly written and lavishly illustrated.

Truth & Lies in Literature by Stephen Vizinczey (University of Chicago). In this collection of essays, the prologue, entitled A Writer's Ten Commandments, advises: "Don't let anybody tell you you're wasting your time when you're gazing into space" – words I take care to remember when engaged in this activity.

The Nation's Favourite Poems (BBC). The result of a poll to discover Britain's favourite poem. It includes poems by Larkin, Donne, Betjeman, Stevie Smith and Jenny Joseph. It's a roll call of beloved poets and I like belonging to the nation that chose them.

Barry Cryer

*Comedy writer Barry Cryer chooses six of his favourite books by J.B. Priestley. Cryer's autobiography, **You Won't Believe This But...**, is published by Virgin Books.*

Issue 178: 7th November 1988

Bright Day (Mandarin). J.B.'s own favourite. With a characteristic "Time" theme, it's the story of an English-born scriptwriter who retreats to a quiet hotel to write a screenplay. There he meets someone who propels him back to his early years in Yorkshire. All the Priestley sweep and scale is here.

Saturn Over The Water (Mandarin). I read this before I fell upon Priestley's best-known books (see Good Companions). It seems forgotten now that he had such an enormous range of style. Almost Bond-like in its unravelling of a world conspiracy, with a dash of sci-fi thrown in. Totally dissimilar to his earlier stories of people thrown together by chance.

Lost Empires (Vintage). Very much in the Good Companions mould, but none the worse for that. Once again, someone is catapulted back in time. An amazing tapestry of music halls, magic and murder. The sheer command of the telling is breathtaking.

Margin Released (Out of print). Although there are several excellent biographies in print, go back to the source. Here it is, in J.B.'s own words, his personal testament. An engrossing insight into the author of the previous five gems.

The Good Companions (Vintage). The chef d'oeuvre and one that those who have never read Priestley have heard of. I discovered this in a bookshop in St Ives and that was the holiday taken care of. A great cosy armchair of a book that envelopes and embraces you.

English Journey (Mandarin). Long before Alan Whicker, Clive James, Michael Palin et al, Priestley was on the road. This book paints a definitive picture of life in England in the early Thirties. The past is a different country and he takes us there.

Theodore Dalrymple

*The journalist known as Theodore Dalrymple is an inner-city doctor. Here he chooses his six best books on medical history. His book, **So Little Done: The Testament of a Serial Killer**, has been re-issued by Ferrington Books.*

Issue 471: 31st July 2004

Medicine and Magnificence by Christine Stevenson (Yale University Press). An absorbing look at the social and artistic background to some of the splendid hospital buildings erected until the principle of utility took over and made everything ugly. I don't think anyone will be writing admiringly of our hospital architecture in 200 years' time.

The White Death: A History of Tuberculosis by Thomas Dormandy (out of print). Once called the Captain of the Men of Death, TB is making a comeback. This is a beautiful history of its effect on the population and also on literature and music. It can be read with the ease of a good novel.

Vincent Van Gogh: Chemicals, Crises and Creativity by Wilfred Niels Arnold (Birkhauser). The story of famous men's illnesses is always interesting. Here is an intriguing, if unproved, biochemical hypothesis concerning Van Gogh's madness.

Narcotic Culture by Frank Dikötter, Lars Laamann and Zhou Xun (C. Hurst & Co). A fascinating revisionist examination of the place of opium in Chinese history. This book attacks the idea that the Chinese were just passive victims of a wicked plot to addict them to opium, and indeed that opium addiction had the socially disastrous consequences often ascribed to it.

The Impact Of Plague in Tudor and Stuart England by Paul Slack (Oxford University Press). There are no end of books about the plague, but this is one of the best. A fine mixture of demographic statistics and imaginative writing.

Laughing Death: The Untold Story of Kuru by Vincent Zigas (Humana). This is the enthralling story of the discovery of the transmission of kuru in New Guinea by the ritual consumption of brains of the dead, the discovery for which Dr Carleton Gajdusek won the Nobel Prize.

William Deedes

*Lord Deedes, the columnist and former editor of The Daily Telegraph, chooses his seven favourite books. His book, **At War with Waugh: The Real Story of "Scoop"**, is published by Macmillan.*

Issue 363: 22nd June 2002

Between Siegfried Sassoon's **Memoirs of a Fox-Hunting Man** and **Memoirs of an Infantry Officer** (Faber & Faber) I can never decide which I like better. The first is a portrait of rural England drawn from the Weald of Kent just before World War I. The second is a portrait of the war itself. It contains the best description written by anybody of the Battle of the Somme. People unfriendly to fox-hunting can pick up the first without a qualm, for it is very gentle prose. And those who detest war will enjoy the second because Siegfried, having won a Military Cross on the Western Front, then delivered a resounding condemnation of the war and temporarily finished up in a psychiatric ward.

A Tale of Two Cities by Charles Dickens (Penguin) Heavy-going in parts, but still a wonderful thriller about the French Revolution with a terrific finish.

Blandings Castle by PG Wodehouse (Penguin) A collection of brilliant short stories focusing on all members of the Emsworth clan. As Evelyn Waugh put it, "the gardens of Blandings Castle are that original garden from which we are exiled".

Scoop by Evelyn Waugh (Picador) A comic novel about reporters in the Abyssinian war of 1935-36. I was there. This book is a must for any would-be foreign correspondents.

My Early Life by Winston Churchill (Eland Books) Published in 1930, at the start of what are called his "wilderness years", this is arguably the best of all his books. It's an attractive portrait of the age in which he grew up, written before the sheer pressure of writing for a living turned him into a literary co-operative.

England, their England by AG Macdonell (Picador) A Scotsman tours England in the Twenties and draws a very jolly portrait of English life between the wars. The account of the village cricket match is particularly amusing.

Colin Dexter

*The novelist Colin Dexter, creator of Inspector Morse, chooses his six favourite detective stories. His last Morse novel, **The Remorseful Day**, is published in paperback by Pan.*

Issue 264: 15th July 2000

A Fatal Inversion by Barbara Vine – Ruth Rendell's alter ego – (Penguin). A psychological thriller which displays the author's exceptionally versatile talent to the full. The great critic F.E. Pardoe puts his money on this being the best crime story of the last 50 years.

The False Inspector Dew by Peter Lovesey (Out of print). An extraordinarily clever, fascinating novel, set aboard a transatlantic liner and loosely based on the Crippen murder case. Compulsively readable. Lovesey has just been awarded the Cartier Diamond Dagger for this millennium year.

The Big Sleep by Raymond Chandler (Penguin). Philip Marlowe is my detective hero, and any of the books would have served (except Playback). But the story here – as evocative, poignant, memorable as the rest – has an ambience all of its own. And what a great title.

And Then There Were None by Agatha Christie (HarperCollins). Many would pick The Murder of Roger Ackroyd as the peak of Christie's achievement. But for me this is the most satisfying of the many puzzles created by that imaginative and ingenious mind.

The Glass Key by Dashiell Hammett (Vintage US). The best novel of the best of the hard-boiled writers, movingly conveying the complexity and precariousness of human relationships. It's also a cracking good read.

The Hollow Man (in the US The Three Coffins) by John Dickson Carr (Chivers Press). One of the most outrageously implausible plots ever, but also the most staggeringly ingenious of Carr's famous "locked room" mysteries.

Josceline Dimbleby

*Cookery writer Josceline Dimbleby chooses her five favourite books. Her book, **A Profound Secret: May Gaskell, Her Daughter Amy, and Edward Burne-Jones**, is published by Doubleday.*

Issue 453: 27th March 2004

The Prince of West End Avenue by Alan Isler (Vintage). I prefer reading about true life but this novel about a Holocaust survivor, as he ends his days in a Jewish old people's home in New York, seems vividly real. A cast of over-eighties put on a production of Hamlet, and the rehearsals bring back old memories, regrets and desires. This is a moving book, full of humour and poignancy.

Toast by Nigel Slater (Fourth Estate). I love Nigel Slater's simple style, and the humorous yet passionate way he looks at things. This story of his lonely childhood, interwoven with and inseparable from food, rings bells for me. A book I didn't want to put down, it is funny, sad and incredibly moving.

Samuel Pepys: The Unequalled Self by Claire Tomalin (Penguin). It is hard to believe that a work of such thorough academic research can make such compulsive reading. Characters and events come alive again and the story is as gripping as a thriller. The detailed evocation of 17th century London is fascinating – after reading this book, I found myself looking at the city I live in with a new eye.

Portrait of a Turkish Family by Irfan Orga (Eland). One of my favourite books; a heartbreaking family saga. It begins with an insight into upper-class life in Istanbul at the start of the 20th century, which was soon to be shattered by the First World War.

The relationship between the author and his father, and the family's descent into penniless hardship, are deeply touching.

Basil Street Blues by Michael Holroyd (Abacus). I read parts of this book over and over again. Holroyd's sense of humour and way of observing the world seem perfect to me. This memoir is as moving as it is humorous, full of warmth yet melancholy. I can't wait to read the follow-up, Mosaic.

J.P. Donleavy

*J.P. Donleavy, the author of The Ginger Man, selects his five favourite books. His novel, **The Lady Who Liked Clean Rest Rooms**, is published by Little, Brown.*

Issue 98: 19th April 1997

Meetings with Remarkable Trees by Thomas Pakenham (Weindenfield & Nicholson). An all-time publishing classic about the kings of horticulture: trees. The kind of work you might expect from this eccentrically cerebral gentleman and celebrated historian, but one is unprepared for its astonishing beauty.

He Had My Heart Scalded by Ernest Gabler (Out of print). If you ever wanted to read about what Dublin was like during World War II, and to be taken down its slum streets with a dozen souls to a room, then read this book. It tells of the utter sadness of an old shackled Ireland.

Both the Lades and the Gentlemen by William Donaldson (Out of print). One of the great British novels on the theme of hypocrisy, which points a sharp finger at the not always edifying character of the English upper class. A work of satiric subtlety that you would expect from the man who is also known as Henry Root, fishmonger.

The Ladies Man by Max Egremont (Out of print). A novel about the people who "took pride in their loneliness": the aristocracy. A haunting portrait of the ordinary moments in lives of elegance and privilege.

The Mullendore Murder Case by Jonathon Kwitney (Out of print). A masterpiece of reportage concerning a Seventies' murder and a life-insurance claim – the largest ever recorded in the history of American underwriting.

Margaret Drabble

*Margaret Drabble, novelist, biographer and editor of **The Oxford Companion to English Literature**, chooses her six favourite books. Her novel, **The Witch of Exmoor**, is published by Penguin.*

Issue 213: 17th July 1999

Heshel's Kingdom by Dan Jacobson (Penguin). This is a remarkable and gripping book about the author's search for his Jewish roots in Lithuania, and his questioning of the miracle of good and bad luck which allowed his own branch of the family to survive. One of the best post-holocaust memoirs, in which every word rings true.

A Scent of Roses by Tim Lott (Penguin). The sad story of Tim Lott's mother, and of his exploration of the inexplicable tragedy of her life and death. Touching, acutely observed, full of social detail, as rich as a novel in colour and psychology. He writes as well about the social significance of a carriage clock as his mother's suicide.

Hidden Lives by Margaret Forster (Penguin) is another family exploration, which uncovers secrets and silences, and mourns the frustrations and sheer physical difficulties of the lives of women of her mother's generation, contrasting them with the freedoms of her own.

The War After: Living with the Holocaust by Anne Karpf (Mandarin). A post-holocaust account of the immigrant experience in London, seen through both first and second generation memories. A keen sociological examination as well as an excellent insight into Karpf's relationship with her over-protective Polish parents.

Under My Skin by Doris Lessing (Flamingo) is an autobiographical volume describing her family background, her childhood in South Africa, her difficult relationship with her mother – painful, honest, exhilarating and unsparing.

In My Own Time: Almost an Autobiography by Nina Bawden (Virago) is an elegant account of the "myths and half-truths of family history", written with an uncanny memory for childhood experience that has made her such a fine writer both for the young and for adults.

Maureen Duffy

*Maureen Duffy, the author, playwright and poet, chooses six books that shaped her writing life. Her book, **Alchemy**, is published in paperback by Harper Perennial.*

Issue 532: 8th October 2005

Herself Surprised by Joyce Cary (New York Review of Books). In this central novel of his triptych Cary brilliantly inhabits the interior voice of his protagonist Sarah Monday, an uneducated housekeeper, as she tries to make sense of her life while in prison for theft, through a miasma of self-deception.

Dubliners by James Joyce (Everyman). Although portraying Dublin at the start of the 20th century these stories are still vivid and fresh. The last, The Dead, is among the finest things Joyce ever wrote. Witty and compassionate as a picture of provincial life, it evokes the depths of human loss and morality.

Oroonoko and Other Stories by Aphra Behn (Penguin). In 1663 Behn went to Surinam and witnessed the events which, 20 years later, she wove into an account of a slave rebellion in which she takes the side of the slaves. Clear-sighted, passionate and told with pace and precise observation.

Between the Acts by Virginia Woolf (Oxford University Press). This lyrical interweaving of a village pageant with the lives of its actors and audience foreshadows our preoccupations with history and identity. The lives of the participants are as fractured as the pageant itself, interrupted by all the disasters of amateur theatricals.

Collected Poems by John Donne (Wordsworth Editions). Still the sexiest poems in or out of the canon, whether he's writing to his mistress or God. Cynical, inquiring, passionate and entirely modern in their expression of naked desire. Try "Come madam, come" for starters.

Ecclesiastical History of the English People by Bede (Penguin). Don't be put off by the title. Our first history book takes our story up to 731, and were he alive today Bede would give Holmes and Schama a run for their money. Full of facts, anecdotes and wisdom. A brilliant picture of distant but still relevant times.

Sarah Dunant

*Sarah Dunant, author and former presenter of BBC's **The Late Show**, chooses her six favourite thrillers. Her novel, **Mapping the Edge**, is published by Warner.*

Issue 278: 21st October 2000

The Talented Mr Ripley by Patricia Highsmith (Random House). Forget the movie, read the book. Dark, amoral, funny, clever and craftily told. I think Highsmith is one of the best thriller writers of the century. She not only knows how to plot, she knows how to write.

The Name of the Rose by Umberto Ecco (Random House). The best thrillers are the ones that thrill intellectually and emotionally. This is one of the best. Murder and mayhem in a medieval monastery, with the inquisition banging on the doors outside. Even if you guess who, you'll never work out why until the end.

Rogue Male by Geoffrey Household (Orion). Household is out of fashion, but he knew how to write thrillers. This is about a secret agent who is pursued through the English countryside after attempting to kill Hitler. The landscape gets darker and darker as the hunt closes in.

The Big Sleep by Raymond Chandler (Penguin). Chandler, the master of pulp crime fiction in the Forties, could be said to have invented the one-liner. The immortal private eye Philip Marlow is hired to protect a general's wild daughter, and finds, several murders later, that he is in love with her sister.

A Philosophical Investigation by Philip Kerr (Vintage). Early use of virtual reality in this nasty but original thriller about a serial killer who sees himself as a philosopher out to rid the world of other serial killers. It features a fabulous female cop with a nice line in put-downs.

A Dark Adapted Eye by Barbara Vine (Penguin). Ruth Rendell is even better as Barbara Vine. It starts with a hanging and gradually digs deeper into the murky depths of family passion to uncover both crime and killer. This novel is both a thriller and a poignant portrait of growing up in postwar Britain.

Ben Elton

*Ben Elton, the author and comedian, chooses six books he enjoyed as a child. His novel, **Dead Famous**, is published in hardback by Bantam Press.*

Issue 336: 8th December 2001

The Narnia Chronicles by C.S. Lewis (Collins). The Harry Potter of my generation, sheer joy. I cannot wait to share them with my children. Some say that Lewis was a Christian propagandist. I say: "So what?"

The Thirty Nine Steps by John Buchan (Penguin). I first encountered this wonderful yarn when my mother read it to us as an ongoing bedtime story. She did all the accents and skipped over the occasional bits of anti-Semitism. As an adult I find it's best read with a whisky on a sleeper to Scotland.

Animal Farm by George Orwell (Penguin). Another book that my mother read to us. In this magical novel, children discover a heart-breaking tale of love and loyalty, adults a bitter lesson in 20th century history.

The Code of the Woosters by P.G. Wodehouse (Penguin). When I was 11 or 12, I had my moment on the road to Damascus. My father gave me my first Wodehouse – Eggs, Beans and Crumpets – and I learnt that there was such a thing as comic perfection. Wodehouse has to be Britain's greatest comic writer.

The Complete Adventures of Sherlock Holmes by Arthur Conan Doyle (Penguin). I read and reread the Sherlock Holmes novels many times, but they never palled. That's because, although the plots were fun, it was the characters and the language that counted.

Our Island Story by H.E. Marshal (Out of print). Though hopelessly out of date even when I was a child (I had my mother's copy from Christmas 1942), this magical book tells history as I think it should be told: as exciting tales of courage and passion to fire a child's imagination.

Richard J. Evans

*Richard J. Evans, Professor of Modern History at Cambridge University, chooses his six favourite history books. His book, **The Coming of the Third Reich**, is published by Penguin/Allen Lane.*

Issue 437: 29th November 2003

Religion and the Decline of Magic by Keith Thomas (Penguin). A ground-breaking study of why people believed in witchcraft, magic and astrology in 16th and 17th century England, and why so few believed in them by the end of the 18th century. Immensely learned, but also hugely enjoyable.

A History of French Passions 1848-1945 by Theodore Zeldin (Clarendon Press). A highly readable dissection of French life and thought from the mid-19th to the mid-20th century, driven by inexhaustible curiosity about human nature and spiced with extraordinary details of the quirks of French people's lives and attitudes.

What is History? by E.H. Carr (Penguin). This brief guide to what historians do remains a classic after more than 40 years. It's full of wit and wisdom, conveying difficult ideas in an entertaining and accessible manner, and offering plenty of controversial theses for the reader to disagree with.

Montaillou by Emmanuel Le Roy Ladurie (Penguin). This account of everyday life and heretical belief in a medieval village is based on records of the Inquisition read against the grain for the incidental details let slip in the villagers' personal testimonies; no other book conveys the realities of living in the Middle Ages with such immediacy.

A People's Tragedy by Orlando Figes (Pimlico). A powerful narrative of Russia's descent into murder and civil war, this book is unsparing in its judgements and breathtaking in its detailed account of the horrors that swept across Europe's largest state in the early 20th century.

The Nazi Seizure of Power by William Sheridan Allen (Out of print). No other book conveys in such detail what it was like for ordinary Germans to live through the death of democracy and the coming of the Third Reich. First published in 1966, it makes excellent use of interviews of those involved, backing them up with extensive research.

Sebastian Faulks

Writer and journalist Sebastian Faulks, author of the highly acclaimed **Birdsong***, chooses six of his favourite books. His novel,* **Charlotte Gray***, is published by Hutchinson.*

Issue 169: 5th September 1998

For the Union Dead by Robert Lowell (Faber). I will never be this unhappy. To watch such unsparing self-examination, ground out with such technical skill in language of such ambitious honesty, is to see in action what Tolstoy listed as the highest human attributes: love, tenderness, poetry and a philosophic, inquiring spirit.

The House on Moon Lake by Francesca Duranti (HarperCollins). This Italian novel of the late Eighties is part ghost story, part morality play, part realistic novel. It is light in texture and easy to read in a beautiful English version. Within a dozen pages, however, you realize you are in for something profoundly unsettling.

The Histories by Tacitus (Penguin). I like this for the density of its style, and the way the terse, epigrammatic verdicts are so well-suited to the trashy politicians they describe. Tacitus was more cynical than any present-day commentator, yet beneath the surface brilliance you feel a tug of truth.

Living by Henry Green (Harvill). The trouble with many so-called "experimental" writers is that they do not deliver the goods. Green's techniques, however, give pleasures and effects unavailable to more traditional writers. Living – plus Loving, Caught and Back – offer intimate reading experiences that can be found in no other novelist.

War and Peace by Leo Tolstoy (Penguin Classics). With its mixture of close-up studies of girlish hysteria and long-range ruminations on historical process, this is a very strange novel indeed. It is also full of transfixing scenes, such as the one in which Prince Andrew, wounded at Austerlitz, loveless and embittered, passes beneath the teenage Natasha's window and hears her singing.

The Aeneid by Virgil (Vintage). Res ipsa loquitur.

Hugh Fearnley-Whittingstall

Hugh Fearnley-Whittingstall, of River Cottage fame, selects six of his favourite books about fish and fishing.

Issue 145: 21st March 1998

Cod by Mark Kurlansky (Jonathan Cape). An elegaic and gripping book which puts forward a case for the humble cod as shaper of world history. It's an environmental lesson too, as biography threatens to become obituary.

Moby Dick by Herman Melville (Penguin Classics). Melville's Captain Ahab is one of literature's great antiheroes. His pursuit of the great white whale is a ripping yarn and a searing treatise on man's immutable need to scratch great itches.

English Seafood Cookery by Richard Stein (Penguin). With his two very watchable TV series, Stein has helped put fish back on the British menu. This is an essential modern manual of seafood cookery – read it, then head immediately for the fishmonger.

Fish, Fishing and the Meaning of Life by Jeremy Paxman (Penguin). Paxo's anthology of angling writing is a fine haul of piscatorial gems – by turns pastoral, practical and thrilling. Essential fare for angling addicts.

The Ladybird Book of Coarse Fishing (Out of print). The one that got me hooked. Published in the Sixties and aimed at children, there's more wisdom in this little book than in a library of modern "how to" fishing guides.

Salar the Salmon by Henry Williamson (Faber). This account of the life of a River Dart salmon is easy to dismiss as an indulgent exer-cise in anthropomorphism, but give yourself over to its fish-eye view of life in the river and the rewards are great.

Sir Ranulph Fiennes

Sir Ranulph Fiennes, the first man to reach both poles, chooses his six favourite books. **Captain Scott**, *his biography of the polar explorer, is published by Hodder & Stoughton.*

Issue 441: 27th December 2003

Desert, Marsh and Mountain by Wilfred Thesiger (Flamingo). Thesiger, who died this year, was the last of the individual and often eccentric traveller-writers of his generation. This book recreates his life in vivid prose and striking photographs. He always sought the remotest mountain, the unspoilt tribe and the place western culture had not yet tainted.

Gormenghast by Mervyn Peake (Vintage). Step aside Tolkien and Rowling, Peake's Gormenghast trilogy rivals both in terms of imaginative other-worlds. He writes English with a wonderful lilt that places words such as lambkin, lacuna and sussurate into his prose where nothing else would do.

The English by Jeremy Paxman (Penguin). Paxman shows his sensitive side in this insightful search for a definition of Englishness. He asks such questions as how a country of football hooligans can have such an astonishingly low murder rate. We are a gloomy lot, but Paxman is hopeful for the nation in the 21st century.

Antarctica Unveiled by David Yelverton (Out of print). The result of a lifetime of fascination with Antarctic history and 15 years of painstaking research, this book is the first to explode the distorted image of Captain Scott invented by character assassin Roland Huntford.

Hitler's Willing Executioners by Daniel Goldhagen (Abacus). Not a happy Christmas choice, but a book that could change any reader's perceptions of humanity. A work of utmost originality and importance, as authoritative as it is explosive.

Heroes and Villains by Gerald Scarfe et al (National Portrait Gallery). This coffee table book goes beneath the trappings of fame to delve into realities of some of our best-loved or hated celebrities of the past seven centuries. A unique collaboration.

65

Barbara Follett

Barbara Follett, MP for Stevenage and founder of Emily's List UK, a network dedicated to helping Labour women get elected to Parliament, chooses her six favourite books written by women.

Issue 148: 11th April 1998

The Golden Notebook by Doris Lessing (HarperCollins). This epic novel is the only one I know which treats politics as an integral part of a woman's life. Like me, Lessing grew up in Africa and again, like me, that continent shaped her political ideas. Perhaps that is why I read it again and again.

Jane Eyre by Charlotte Brontë (Penguin). Another book I repeatedly turn to. Brontë flouted the conventions of her day by writing this book and Jane also challenges tradition with admirable zeal. Her clear-sighted independence in the face of terrible adversity is an inspiration.

The Second Sex by Simone de Beauvoir (Vintage). I read this mammoth work shortly after I had my first child and it helped me make sense of my confused anger at society's treatment of women.

The Feminine Mystique by Betty Friedan (Penguin). Written in 1963 at the height of the short-lived professional homemaker phase of women's economic history, this book asked out loud the questions millions of women of the time whispered to themselves at their kitchen sinks: "Is this all?"

Pride and Prejudice by Jane Austen (Penguin). A beautifully written, perfectly balanced piece of work. Just like a Bach cantata but with a feisty heroine and a wonderfully sexy hero.

Fear of Flying by Erica Jong (Mandarin). Another first, this time in its treatment of women's sexuality. It made me, and thousands of other women of my generation, feel better about ourselves.

Ken Follett

*Author Ken Follett selects six of his favourite thrillers. His book, **The Third Twin**, is published by Pan.*

Issue 122: 4th October 1997

The Mask of Dimitrios by Eric Ambler. At a party, a mystery writer is approached by a policeman who says: "I don't suppose you'd be interested in a real murder?" This is the beginning of a clever and intricate story that ranges all over Europe between the wars. A classic.

Get Shorty by Elmore Leonard. His unique writing style, colloquial and laconic, is perfectly married to his deadpan stories about American lowlifes clinging to the last shreds of honour and self-respect. This one is also a great film.

The Silence of the Lambs by Thomas Harris. This may be the greatest thriller ever. Unbearably gripping, plausible, grisly, with an appealing detective and a terrifying villain. I wish I had written it.

From Russia with Love by Ian Fleming. I started reading James Bond books at the age of twelve, and it changed my life. This one is my favourite. A beautiful Russian agent falls in love with the photograph of Bond in the file kept on him by the KGB.

The Day of the Jackal by Frederick Forsyth. The best ever cat-and-mouse thriller, so chockablock with authentic detail that you believe in it even though you know that de Gaulle was not assassinated.

Stamboul Train by Graham Greene. I love train stories. This one is set aboard the Orient Express in the twenties. Greene's thrillers are short on action, but their matter-of-fact air makes them very realistic, and of course, they are rather well written.

Frederick Forsyth

*The author Frederick Forsyth chooses five of his favourite history books. His novel, **Avenger**, is published by Bantam Press.*

Issue 424: 30th August 2003

Rise and Fall of the Third Reich by William Schirer (Arrow). Like it or loathe it, the Third Reich is still with us. Print and film industries bombard us with more and more about Hitler, the Nazis and WWII. But how on earth did this talentless drop-out from Braunau actually do it? Schirer explains the greatest crime and the greatest con-trick of our times.

The man and the book are derided because of the flaws in both. But the sheer canvas of **Seven Pillars of Wisdom** by T.E. Lawrence (Penguin) confounds the cynics. He was a remarkable man and he told a remarkable story, filmed by David Lean as one of the greatest movies of the past century.

The Empire Trilogy by Jan Morris (Out of print). Another vast subject, needing three volumes. But Morris, a world-travelled foreign correspondent, sets it all in context; the saints and sinners, heroes and villains, explorers, missionaries, mercenaries, pirates, statesmen, diplomats, doctors and soldiers who made and inhabited for three hundred years this awesome canvas, the British Empire.

Fifteen years ago I asked the SIS's Controller of Western Hemisphere what he foresaw as the supreme danger to us all in the decades after Communism. He didn't pause and used one word: "Proliferation". And now he is proved right. Weapons of mass destruction in the hands of madmen (discovered in Iraq, or not) are the nightmare for the rest of our lives. **Critical Mass** by William Burrows and Robert Windrem (cancelled in advance of publication) explains how and why.

Wellington: Years of the Sword and Pillar of State by Elizabeth Longford (Out of print). I happen to think he was one of the small handful of the eternally "great" – an over-used word. The late Lady Longford brings him alive, talents and faults, from the depths of despair to the pinnacle at Waterloo, and always with his own wry, sardonic humour.

Nick Foulkes

The author Nick Foulkes chooses five books that convey a vivid sense of time and place. His own book, **Last of the Dandies – The Scandalous Life and Escapades of Count D'Orsay***, is published by Little, Brown.*

Issue 421: 9th August 2003

Vanity Fair by W.M. Thackeray (Penguin). Thackeray's scathing contempt for all aspects of polite society is so refreshing: pretensions are pitilessly exposed and mercilessly mocked. It provides a colourful picture of life before the crushing morality of Victoria's England took all the fun out of the 19th century.

The First Circle by Aleksandr Solzhenitsyn (Northwestern University Press). To describe this as a novel about a long weekend in a Soviet prison camp is to say that Romeo and Juliet is a play about a teenage crush. The First Circle is a genuine work of genius; Solzhenitsyn compresses the whole experience of Stalin's Russia into this extraordinary book.

The Reminiscences and Recollections of Captain Gronow by R.H. Gronow (Out of print). When I was working on my biography of Count d'Orsay, I found myself warming to a diminutive Welsh soldier, dandy and society figure called Rees Howell Gronow, whose memoirs recall the best bits of life in the first half of the 19th century.

The Comedians by Graham Greene (Vintage). Greene captured the absurdity of life in the 20th century, the declining influence of the old European world and that strange listlessness that results – wandering about the more recondite corners of Cuba or the Dominican Republic it is still possible to pick up a whiff of the world he wrote about. The Comedians has it all: comedy, tragedy, pathos, the Caribbean, and an almost Ian Fleming-like eye for detail.

Lincoln by Gore Vidal (Abacus). It took me a little while to get the hang of Vidal's novels, nevertheless I can recommend the historical sextet that he calls Narratives of a Golden Age by saying that they're an extremely painless way to find out about American history. Although part of this sequence – his history of the Lincoln presidency – stands alone and can be read as such.

James Fox

*The author James Fox chooses five books for their exceptional reconstruction of time and place. His book, **The Langhorne Sisters**, is published by Granta.*

Issue 203: 8th May 1999

Death in Paris 1795-1801 by Richard Cobb (Out of print). A state mortician's dossier of 400 violent deaths near the Seine – mostly suicides – enables Cobb to display his unrivalled knowledge of the Revolutionary period. From details of clothes, pockets, ragbag possessions, even the bridges they jumped from, he mesmerically revives the brutal life of the poor of his favourite city, barely recovered from the Terror.

News of a Kidnapping by Gabriel Garcia Marquez (Penguin). In 1990 Pablo Escobar, drug king of Medellin, kidnapped ten prominent Colombians. Marquez – in "the saddest and most difficult task of my life" – reconstructs from the accounts of those who survived the three and a half years of terror and negotiation with the government that ended in Escobar's bizarre surrender.

The Other Garden by Francis Wyndham (Out of print). An extraordinary evocation of marginal characters in a Marlborough village forced together by the war – with a precise ear for their talk, snobbery and manners. It tells of the poignant effect of romantic friendship on the author – a tubercular young conscript – with an alienated local girl. A document of a genteel, lost world revived decades later in perfect prose and with hilarious irony.

With Napoleon in Russia – The Memoirs of General Caulaincourt, Duke of Vicenza (Constable). Caulaincourt had a world scoop in 1812 when Napoleon chose him as his companion on the journey back from Moscow to Paris, ahead of the bad news. Breathtaking recorded dialogue of Boney's denial of the coming winter.

Captain James Cook by Richard Hough (Hodder). Biography as thriller. The labourer's son from Yorkshire ventures into the equivalent of outer space in wooden boats. A fluent, vivid, deeply entertaining account of this brilliant man and his friends from the diaries they kept.

Dick Francis

*The bestselling author Dick Francis chooses his six favourite books. His novel, **Second Wind**, is published by Michael Joseph.*

Issue 219: 28th August 1999

Reflections in a Silver Spoon: A Memoir by Paul Mellon (John Murray). Paul Mellon was one of the 20th century's greatest philanthropists. He was a great scholar and art collector and had a passion for horse racing. He owned horses which won both the Epsom and Kentucky Derbys as well as thousands of other major races all around the world.

The Calendar by Edgar Wallace (Out of print). Edgar Wallace was a genius of suspense writing and he was a great influence on my own work. The Calendar is one of his best and I believe it to be the greatest racing mystery ever written.

Bomber Command by Max Hastings (Macmillan). Hastings's account of the bomber war in Europe between 1940 and 1945 is of particular interest to me as I was a pilot during much of that time. Only after the event does one realise the part played in the wider strategy.

Fred Archer by John Welcome (Out of print). Archer was a genius jockey in the late 19th century, who rode over 200 winners a season. He was a manic-depressive who, at six foot tall, had constantly to starve himself to ride. He killed himself at the age of 29 but not before he became the sports celebrity of his time.

Men and Horses I Have Known by the Hon. George Lampton (J.A. Allen & Co). An autobiography of one of the great racehorse trainers and characters of the past century. This work recalls the major changes in racing during his time and makes one ever conscious of how the influence of such men has moulded the Sport of Kings as we know it today.

The Spirit of St Louis by Charles Lindbergh (Out of print). The story of one man's determination to succeed against the odds, recalled by the aviator himself. Leaves one on the edge of one's seat.

Jonathan Freedland

Author and columnist Jonathan Freedland chooses his six favourite books on Israel and the Middle East.

Issue 402: 29th March 2003

The Iron Wall by Avi Shlaim (Penguin). In a conflict as fraught as this one, the past is no less controversial than the present, which makes a clear-eyed, sober account like Shlaim's all the more welcome. With access to once-closed archives, Shlaim cuts through the myths. Essential.

One Palestine Complete by Tom Segev (Abacus). A vast, exhilarating survey of the years when Palestine was ruled by Britain. Interweaving the memories of individuals with the larger history of a great power and two national movements, Segev dispels some of the legends he and his fellow Israelis were raised on – and gives a new perspective on the British Empire itself.

In the Land of Israel by Amos Oz (Out of print). Written in the aftermath of the Lebanon war and now 20 years old, Oz's journey through his country is still a classic. Oz met everyone – Palestinians, Jews on both the Left and Right, settlers on the West Bank and immigrants from North Africa – and let them speak in their own voice.

The Yellow Wind by David Grossman (Out of print). Oz's fellow novelist made a similar quest, but concentrated on the occupied territories. Grossman's book presented Israelis with a truth they had not wanted to face. In exquisite prose, he gets to the heart of two peoples locked in mortal combat.

The Question of Palestine by Edward Said (Out of print). Said has done more than anybody else to bring the Palestinian plight to the attention of the world. This book gives a direct account – infused with personal experience – of how Israel's birth in 1948 entailed liberty for one nation and catastrophe for another.

From Beirut to Jerusalem by Thomas L. Friedman (HarperCollins). Many years ago, the New York Times columnist was a foreign correspondent, first in Lebanon and then in Israel. His eye for the telling anecdote and human story makes this an ideal outsider's perspective on a troubled region.

Dawn French

The comedienne and actress Dawn French chooses six of her favourite books.

Issue 154: 23rd May 1998

Decline and Fall by Evelyn Waugh (Penguin). Quite simply the funniest book I've ever read, and the only book I've read more than once. The other Waugh books are a bit of a disappointment after this.

The Idea of the American South (1920-1941) by M. O'Brien (John Hopkins University Press, out of print). Not many laughs here, but a surprisingly accessible book which offers a new perspective on American history. It was written by my uncle, who is very clever, and who sports the largest sideburns in modern history.

Just the Beginning by Robson Green (Boxtree). This book has not left my bedside since my birthday last year, when a true friend gave it to me as a gift. There are a load of delicious snaps and important information – but, for my money, there's not enough pictures of him without a shirt. Perhaps the next installment could be "Just The Middle".

Captain Corelli's Mandolin by Louis de Bernières (Minerva). It's utterly enchanting. A fascinating mixture of comedy and tragedy; a feast for all the senses. I'm so glad I read it.

If He Lives by J.S. Fink (Vintage). A frightening and touching modern ghost story. The ghost creeps in through the chinks in the marriage. The writer is known to me and is unfeasibly attractive.

Green Eggs and Ham by Dr Seuss (HarperCollins). This is the book that made my daughter want to read. The most requested pre-bedtime read in our house. Weird, funny and good.

Esther Freud

The author Esther Freud chooses her six favourite books.
*Her novel, **The Sea House**, is published by Hamish Hamilton.*

Issue 422: 16th August 2003

Anna Karenina by Leo Tolstoy (Penguin). This is probably my all-time favourite novel. It satisfies on every level with its humour, philosophy and romance. When I think of the inter-weaving stories of Anna, Kitty and Levin, and the St Petersburg gentlemen's clubs, I can see it as clearly as if each page were a reel of film.

The Pursuit of Love by Nancy Mitford (Penguin). This is a perfect book. Its subject is a large, chaotic family, based in part on Mitford's own, brought to life with such love, delicacy and wit that it makes you want to crawl into the "Hons cup-board" and eavesdrop on everything they have to say.

The Slow Train To Milan by Lisa St Aubin de Terán (Out of print). This is another book about a girl's coming-of-age story, but told in such an eccentric, unusual and hysterically funny way that it makes you want to take off for Italy yourself, preferably by train, so that you can stop at random stations along the way.

Jane Eyre by Charlotte Brontë (Penguin). Jane Eyre is the study of someone who is more courageous than anyone expects her to be. And, of course, it is dizzyingly romantic. How often as a teenager did I lean out of a window hoping to actually hear a Mr Rochester calling my name?

What a Carve Up by Jonathan Coe (Penguin). Coe's subjects are factory farming, arms dealing, the declining health service, and the life of a failed writer. It's as if he had enough material for five books, but generously packed them into one. For me this was the most ambitious and successful book of the Nineties.

Voyage in the Dark by Jean Rhys (Penguin). It's a deceptively simple novel, short and immensely readable. It follows the story of a young actress, alone and adrift in London. And although it was written in the Thirties, there is nothing dated about this story of first love, and the fickleness of its players.

Mariella Frostrup

Mariella Frostrup, journalist and broadcaster, chooses six of her favourite books to catch up with on holiday.

Photo: Frank Bauer

Issue 320: 18th August 2001

The Moor's Last Sigh by Salman Rushdie (Vintage). A tragicomic tale of the disintegrating fortunes of a dynastic Bombay family, as told through the eyes of their crossbreed son Moracs (hence the Moor). A loving portrait of a vanishing world, this rich feast of language, storytelling and mischievous word-play is Rushdie at his brilliant best.

Naples '44 by Norman Lewis (Eland Books). An account of a year spent amid the bedlam of wartime Naples by one of the very few great travel writers working today. It's a wonderful portrait of the city's notorious small-time crooks, laced with wry observations on the day-to-day realities of wartime living.

The War of Don Emmanuel's Nether Parts by Louis de Bernières (Minerva). I laughed all the way through de Bernières' playful homage to South America's long tradition of magic realism. His description of the eponymous hero's ride into town on his obstinate horse had tears streaming down my face.

Into The Heart Of Borneo by Redmond O'Hanlon (Macmillan). An incongruous blend of comic observation and Victorian- style exploration, this is a wonderful real-life adventure story. The eccentric O'Hanlon, by his own admission an unfit Oxford don, makes an unlikely yet intrepid hero.

Cloudstreet by Tim Winton (Picador). Two Melbourne families are forced to share a crumbling house on Cloud Street. As the years pass by, their forced proximity provides a joyous lesson in tolerance, survival and the transforming power of love.

Tourist Season by Carl Hiaasen (Pan). Pulp fiction at its best. The first and my favourite in Hiaasen's blackly comic series of novels about the decimation of Florida by big business, mass tourism and lowlife crime. This is a hilarious tale about an incompetent terrorist group who set out to rid their beloved state of the menace of tourism.

75

Frances Fyfield

*Frances Fyfield, the crime novelist and criminal lawyer, chooses six books that depict kindness alongside cruelty. Her book, **Looking Down**, is published by Time Warner Books.*

Issue 480: 2nd October 2004

My Name Is Legion by A.N. Wilson (Arrow). Wilson can write across all disciplines. This is his first novel for a while, and it's a wonderful, thrilling depiction of media manipulation, corruption, tolerance and promiscuity. It's so good, and so wise, it hurts. It's the late-20th century in a gulp.

A Big Boy Did it and Ran Away by Christopher Brookmyre (Abacus). Thriller in which a failing teacher meets up with an old school friend, now turned terrorist, and so begins a rollercoaster ride of bomb evasion. Tells you more about courage and the real nature of terrorism than any journalist.

Being Dead by Jim Crace (Penguin). A middle-aged couple go for a nostalgic walk on the sand dunes. They are killed, and this extraordinary novel plots the courses of their lives through the physical decay of their bodies, somehow making sense of both. A terrifying, scientific love poem by an author of fantastic, lyrical imagination.

The American Boy by Andrew Taylor (HarperCollins). This book features the young Edgar Allen Poe and his teacher, but the real theme is the cruelty of the inequality of the age; and the key question is how the individual combats it – in any age, including now.

Death in Holy Orders by P.D. James (Penguin). James's thoughtful and wise depiction of the stresses of the monastic life. She is extraordinarily adept at what makes good people resort to evil, horribly controlled in her descriptions of violence, and knows where the bodies are buried.

The Anglo-Irish Murders by Ruth Dudley Edwards (Out of print). The penultimate of RDE's oeuvre of satirical novels, quite different from her series of documentary histories. This is a gloriously funny send-up of Anglo-Irish relations, set at a Cultural Conference where the participants would rather murder (as they do) than agree.

Timothy Garton Ash

*The contemporary historian and political writer Timothy Garton Ash chooses his six favourite books. His book, **Free World: Why a Crisis of the West Reveals the Opportunity of Our Time**, is published by Penguin.*

Issue 461: 22nd May 2004

Robert Browning Poems. The English poet to whom I always return. He engages wonderfully with different times and places, especially in Latin Europe, but the truths extracted are universal. Love Among the Ruins should be read at least once a month by anyone who is inclined to be impressed by worldly glory.

Redgauntlet by Walter Scott (Oxford University Press). Scott wrote a fair amount of tosh, but his finest historical novels, such as Redgauntlet, have tremendous energy, scale and drama. Here, he invents a third Jacobite rising against the House of Hannover. Like Browning, he is brilliant at commingling the personal and the political.

Homage to Catalonia by George Orwell (Penguin). A gold standard for writing about a foreign crisis. Anything written on Vietnam, Bosnia or Iraq has to be measured against it. Orwell fought in the trenches for the Republican side, and was shot through the neck. Yet he came back and wrote an account which reserved its fiercest criticism for his own team, the Left. Valiant-for-Truth with a typewriter.

Radical Chic by Tom Wolfe (Pan Macmillan). Amazing that a piece of journalism more than 30 years old and very bound to its time can still be so enjoyable today. But it is. Like all great satire, it leaps beyond time and place.

Essays by Thomas Babington Macaulay. Macaulay's historical, political and literary essays are models of style and treasure-caves of learning. And he can be gloriously rude: "We have, for some time past, observed the strange infatuation which leads the Poet Laureate to abandon those departments of literature in which he might excel... He has, we think, done his worst."

Gedichte by Goethe (Insel Verlag). Does anyone read him now? Goethe breathes a spirit of Enlightenment humanism that is the best of the West. And he puts the best words in the best order.

Bamber Gascoigne

Bamber Gascoigne, a former presenter of University Challenge, has written an interactive world history for the internet that can be found at **www.historyworld.net***. Here, he chooses five favourite works of reference.*

Issue 318: 4th August 2001

Whitaker's Almanack (Stationery Office Books). A treasure trove of topical information about Britain and the world, and one not widely enough appreciated. I buy each new edition and the volumes now fill two shelves. I can find out instantly the correct detail in any year during the recent decades.

Book of Rock Stars by Dafydd Rees (Guinness World Records). I know nothing about rock stars, but I once needed information about them for a project and so came across this amazing compilation. It charts the adventures of the stars and their groups week by week, month by month. An amazing labour of love. Sounds awful but you soon become absorbed.

Encyclopedia Britannica. During the 25 years in which I presented University Challenge, and more recently while writing HistoryWorld, I spent much of my time with my nose in reference books. Britannica is undoubtedly the granddaddy of all English-language works of reference, invaluable on every subject. But it has to be said that it is very much better in printed form than on the internet.

The Oxford Companion to Children's Literature by Humphrey Carpenter and Mari Prichard (Oxford University Press). This is one of the best-planned and executed reference books that I have come across. Written in delightful detail, the book anticipates everything that one might want to look up on the subject – and guides one unerringly to the right entry.

The Good Opera Guide by Sir Denis Forman (Weidenfeld & Nicolson). A guide to the best-known operas by someone who knows them well. The author is illuminating about the music and shamelessly funny at the expense of the plots. Not for the over-solemn. But if you like opera and enjoy irreverence, you will have a wonderful time.

Victoria Glendinning

*Victoria Glendinning, the biographer and novelist, chooses her six favourite books. Her novel, **Flight**, is published by Scribner.*

Issue 400: 15th March 2003

Being Dead by Jim Crace (Penguin). Crace's writing is like no one else's. This frighteningly original and moving novel is the story of a marriage – told in retrospect, as the corpses of the spouses graphically decompose. But the timelessness and tenderness of love redeem the flesh's rot.

The Burning of Bridget Cleary: A True Story by Angela Bourke (Pimlico). Brilliantly researched and narrated, this tells the story of a young wife in Tipperary who died at home one night in 1895. Were the fairies involved in her violent death? Around this notorious story winds a disturbingly fascinating investigation into the bizarre effects of all irrational belief systems.

Life & Times of Michael K by J.M.Coetzee (Minerva). A handicapped man, with his dying mother in a handcart, starts on a hopeless journey from Cape Town to her home village, assailed by civil strife and the malice of strangers. This Eighties Booker winner is an inspired, inspirational feat of empathy.

Gulliver's Travels by Jonathan Swift (Penguin). Most people read a sanitised version in childhood, though children would love the lavatory humour that sluices through the original. Never has the futility of politics and warmongering, the ludicrousness of dogma, doctrine, human irrationality and greed, been so savagely and enjoyably laid bare.

Burmese Days by George Orwell (Penguin). A tougher, funnier version of Forster's Passage to India, about the maverick Flory's disastrous efforts to bridge the gulf between the locals and their British rulers. The scheming Burmese officials are awful. But for sheer nastiness, nothing can touch the British administrators.

The Blue Flower by Penelope Fitzgerald (Flamingo). Clever, idealistic Fritz (a real person, the poet Novalis) falls irrevocably in love with sickly, stupid, 12-year-old Sophie. The novel deals unforgettably with overwhelming passion, while inhabiting 18th century domestic life as if by magic. Historical fiction was never like this.

Simon Gray

*The author Simon Gray had six teeth extracted. These are the books he laid out for his return from hospital. His memoirs, **The Smoking Diaries**, are published in paperback by Granta Books.*

Issue 501: 5th March 2005

The Diary of a Nobody by George and Weedon Grossmith (Oxford University Press). Not only because it's funny and touching, but also because I feel that Pooter is a kindred spirit, heroic, stoical and misunderstood, whose jokes are even worse than mine, and his pride in them even greater.

Required Writing by Philip Larkin (Faber & Faber) because his voice – decent, humane and reflective – is one of the few I'd like to have in my ear when nursing a sore jaw. I'd go straight to his essays on Betjeman, in which you feel England lost twice over, both his and Betjeman's a world away from ours (although on the moral calendar we seem only to have got to 1984).

The Papers of A.J. Wentworth, BA, edited by H.F. Ellis (Prion Books). Wentworth, a direct and noble descendant of Pooter, is a prep school teacher from a prelapsarian age – the Forties, minus the War – who struggles daily, like me, to preserve his self-esteem in a downwardly mobile world.

Vintage Thurber: A Selection of the Best Writings and Drawings of James Thurber: Vols I & II (Out of print). Because Thurber's prose is soothing, charming and funny, his cartoons witty and his drawings, particularly of dogs, enchanting.

Four Quartets by T.S. Eliot (Faber & Faber) should the operation prove to be a near-death experience. Finally, in case I should feel an urge to return to work before health and morale are fully restored, I'd have the first of my own diaries,

An Unnatural Pursuit (Faber, probably out of print), an account of a failed attempt to transfer a play to the West End – it would remind me of how a great deal of effort, hope and fear can come to nothing, so why bother?

Lloyd Grossman

Loyd Grossman, the television broadcaster and chairman of the Campaign For Museums, here selects his six favourite books for reading and re-reading on the beach.

Issue 110: 12th July 1997

Can Jane Eyre Be Happy? by John Sutherland (Oxford University Press). Amusing and stimulating lit. crit. elegantly unravelling literary conundra; it explains, for example, why Robinson Crusoe found only a single footprint and where Fanny Hill stashed her contraceptives.

Worldly Goods by Lisa Jardine (Macmillan). I applaud the revival of history writing and, ever-curious about the Renaissance (about which I feel I can never know enough), look forward immensely to this book. It gets across the idea that the Renaissance was about more than just perspective and classical scholarship.

Nana by Emile Zola (Penguin). For me, the best ever study of moral bankruptcy and a glittering portrait of Second Empire France. I read it every other year: more fun, less grim, but no less profound than Zola's other novels.

Ben and Me by Robert Lawson (Little, Brown). A fictional biography of Benjamin Franklin – one of my cultural heroes – written from the perspective of his pet mouse, Amos. Mischievous, insightful and full of laughs. Originally published in 1939, I shall read it to my children.

Match the Hatch of the Southern Chalkstreams by Grace Everett (Grace Everett). One of the most useful books recently published for fly fishers. I shall use it to remember all the ones that got away from me while fishing in May and June.

The Red Sox Reader edited by Dan Riley (Houghton Mifflin). An indispensable anthology of the best writing about my team The Boston Red Sox, perpetual losers with style and grace, and the greatest baseball team in the history of the universe.

Joanne Harris

*Joanne Harris, author of the bestselling novel **Chocolat**, chooses six books that she regularly revisits. Her book, **Coastliners**, is published in paperback by Black Swan.*

Issue 390: 28th December 2002

The Gormenghast Trilogy by Mervyn Peake (Vintage). Peake is a writer you either love or hate. I reread this once a year because it is so funny and well written. I fell in love with it when I was a teenager and still am, because it just gets better as you get older and are able to read new things into it.

Lord of the Flies by William Golding (Faber and Faber). I studied this at school, which might have killed a lesser book, but not this one. The savagery of it, the merciless cruelty of the children, seemed so true and eerily familiar (only adults believe their children are innocent) that I read it on the day it was given to me, staying up till two in the morning to finish.

Fahrenheit 451 by Ray Bradbury (Flamingo). I think Bradbury is a brilliant and much underrated author. One of the joys of his work is the vigour with which he writes. As well as being prose-poetry of the purest kind, his books are alive and vibrant and full of fun, a poke in the eye to book-burners and sceptics everywhere.

Salammbô by Gustave Flaubert (Penguin). Readers of Flaubert's Madame Bovary may not be as familiar with this earlier work. It is a magnificently flawed flight of fantasy – like Rider Haggard gone mad – and is full of rampaging warlords, sacred serpents, holy virgins and human sacrifice.

Lolita by Vladimir Nabokov (Penguin). This is the most wonderfully written novel. Nabokov is a perfect linguist and his portrayal of a poet tortured by his obsession for a 12-year-old girl hits the note so well every time.

A Rose for Ecclesiastes by Roger Zelazny (Out of print). A volume of four perfect novellas. Zelazny is a marvellous but underrated writer whose short stories strike a strong human chord.

Lord Harris

Lord Harris of High Cross was an adviser to Margaret Thatcher and is Founder President of the Institute of Economic Affairs. Here he chooses his six favourite books.

Issue 114: 9th August 1997

Three Men in a Boat by Jerome K. Jerome (Penguin). Hilarious re-creation of a Victorian boating holiday on the Thames from Kingston to Oxford by three bachelors. No sex, crime, politics, media. Just comic stories, companionship – and nostalgia.

Bright Promises, Dismal Performance by Milton Friedman (T. Horton, USA). Scintillating collection of Newsweek essays by the foremost economic expositor of the century. What's your problem: inflation, state education, unemployment, taxation, social security, the future? Ask Uncle Milt.

Hayek on Hayek, edited by Kresge and Wenar (Routledge). Charming autobiographical fragment by the most seminal economist / social philosopher since Adam Smith. Revealing glimpses: from childhood in Vienna to LSE, Cambridge and Chicago.

Self Help by Samuel Smiles (IEA). Inspiring gallery of vivid pen portraits which remind us of the inexhaustible reserves of invention, perseverance and achievement waiting to be evoked in often unlikely characters. A perfect antidote to bishops' bleats and party politicians' pretensions.

Savoy Operas by W. S. Gilbert (Wordsworth). An unending river of innocent merriment... Indeed it comprises a self-contained anthology of witty wisdom and incomparable rhyming verse. Every chorus conjures up Sullivan's airs.

Thinking the Unthinkable by Richard Cockett (Fontana). Example of newish art of "contemporary history" reporting, it includes the war between Hayek and the Keynesians, fought mostly by intellectual artillery of "think-tanks" since 1945. Happy ending? Watch Tony Blair!

Robert Harris

The writer Robert Harris chooses his six favourite novels.
*His book, **Pompeii**, is published by Arrow.*

Issue 492: 24th December 2004

Great Expectations by Charles Dickens (Penguin). A novel embodying all Dickens's strengths and none of his weaknesses. Wonderfully realised characters, vividly memorable scenes (the convict in the cemetery, the jilted bride and her decaying wedding breakfast) and a plot as simple and powerful as Greek tragedy.

The Secret Agent by Joseph Conrad (Oxford University Press). Uncannily perceptive in its treatment of the mentality of terrorism. Here, in a novel published in 1907, is our modern world: state sponsors of terrorism, politically pressured intelligence officers, and suicide bombers mingling with crowds of shoppers.

The Quiet American by Graham Greene (Vintage). If Conrad anticipated one half of today's world war – the terrorists – Greene dissected the other half: the blundering, well-meaning, ham-fisted, over-confident, under-informed United States. I wish every CIA officer in the Middle East had a copy of this novel of Vietnam.

1984 by George Orwell (Penguin). Surely the most influential novel ever written. Orwell's ambition was to raise political writing to the level of art, and I can't think of any author whose language and inventions have so deeply penetrated popular consciousness, and reshaped the way we think about power.

The Loved One by Evelyn Waugh (Penguin). Mercilessly bleak and yet wonderfully funny novella lacerating everything Waugh loathed about the modern world. Reactionaries often make the best satirists, and Waugh ranks with Pope and Swift as one of the great, classical English stylists.

Satyricon by Petronius (Hackett). Written almost 2,000 years ago, yet with entirely recognisable characters, plus some very good jokes. At least as daring and experimental as anything produced in modern times: a haunting link with a vanished world which existed 60 generations ago, and proof that words outlast everything else.

Adam Hart-Davis

*Adam Hart-Davis, author, scientist and broadcaster – whose programmes include What the Victorians Did For Us – chooses his six favourite books. His book, **Why Does A Ball Bounce?**, is published by Ebury Press.*

Issue 534: 22nd October 2005

The Formation Of Vegetable Mould Through The Action Of Worms, With Observations On Their Habits by Charles Darwin, (Kessinger Publishing). To investigate their hearing, Darwin got his children to whistle to the worms, and play the piano and the bassoon; he concluded they were deaf, and yet they showed some intelligence.

Winter Holiday by Arthur Ransome (Random House). My dad, who was his friend and editor, claimed that Ransome made detailed notes for the whole of each Swallows & Amazons book, and then started with the chapter he thought would be easiest to write. The best bits are about the ice-yachts and the rescue of the crag-bound sheep.

The Singing Sands by Josephine Tey (Out of print). My mum introduced me to Josephine Tey (along with Dorothy Sayers and others) and this one I find particularly haunting, especially the Scottish vignettes of Wee Archie and the dreadful breakfast in the Western Isles.

The Spy Who Came In From the Cold by John le Carré (Hodder & Stoughton). Le Carré is the master of murky espionage, especially in Tinker, Tailor, Soldier, Spy and Smiley's People, but this, the first one I read, was a superb antidote to the James Bond-style of spy story that became popular in the early sixties.

Rendezvous with Rama by Arthur C. Clarke (Time Warner). Although his characters can be a bit wooden, Sir Arthur has a phenomenal ability to tell a tale just far enough from reality to keep me spooked and yet so logical that I feel he might almost have been there and seen it.

A Brief History of Time by Stephen Hawking (Transworld). I got hold of this on the day of publication and was captivated, although I can understand neither the whole of chapter 6, nor why it has sold in such prodigious numbers.

Max Hastings

*Max Hastings, ex-editor of the Evening Standard, selects his favourite novels. Paperback editions of three of his military histories (**Onslaught**, **Bomber Command** and **The Korean War**) were reissued by Pan.*

Issue 124: 18th October 1997

The Acceptance World by Anthony Powell (Mandarin) Arguably the best of the peacetime novels in the Dance sequence – first hints of Widmerpool as a formidable operator rather than a mere absurdity.

Framley Parsonage by Anthony Trollope (Penguin) Most delightful of the Barchester books, recounting the troubles of young parson Mark Robarts and love life of his sister Lucy. Introduces Rev Josiah Crawley, whose later misfortunes are the focus of the triumphant Last Chronicle.

Flying Colours by CS Forester (Admiral Hornblower Omnibus Penguin). Hornblower's dashing escape from Napoleonic France by the master whom some neglect in favour of Patrick O'Brien. I adore O'Brien, but would never break faith with the endlessly resourceful Hornblower. No wonder the books were Churchill's favourite leisure reading in the war.

Cork On The Water by Macdonald Hastings (Out of print). My father wrote a series of thrillers starring a bowler-hatted insurance company chairman, all set in rural parts and involving mad squires, war veterans, rods and shotguns. I was always captivated by Mr Cork's fantasy world, and the books have never lost their charm as period pieces.

Selina Hastings

The biographer Selina Hastings chooses her six favourite reference books.
*Her book, **Rosamond Lehmann: A Life**, is published by Chatto & Windus.*

Issue 371 17th August 2002

The Reader's Companion to Twentieth Century Writers and The Reader's Companion to the Twentieth Century Novel (Fourth Estate). In my line of business (the writing of literary biography) these two wonderfully readable volumes, edited by Peter Parker, are invaluable reference books.

Kelly's Handbook to the Titled, Landed and Official Classes (Kelly's Directories). Kelly's Handbook is long out of print but eagerly sought after in second-hand bookshops for its rich trove of forgotten brigadier-generals and dowagers living with unmarried daughters in Hyde Park Gate.

Titles and Forms of Address (Adam & Charles Black). This will guide you on the correct way to refer to everyone from marquesses and archdeacons to the children of the widows of the younger sons of barons.

The Oxford Dictionary of the Christian Church edited by F.L. Cross (Oxford University Press). While I was working on the life of Evelyn Waugh this dictionary came regularly to my rescue, explaining all the ontology, teleology and epistemology that I needed to have at my fingertips.

Handbook of Dates for Students of English History ed. by C.R. Cheney (Cambridge University Press). The hideous task of trying]to date undated correspondence is made much easier by this magical little book with its lists of saints' days and Easter Day tables.

Chambers Biographical Dictionary edited by Magnus Magnusson (Chambers). This dictionary is another useful tool. When I come across a famous name about whom I know nothing, I look it up here and in a few succinct lines find all I need.

Roy Hattersley

*Roy Hattersley, author and former Deputy Leader of the Labour Party, chooses his five favourite books. His book, **The Edwardians**, is published by Little, Brown.*

Issue 482: 16th October 2004

Far From the Madding Crowd by Thomas Hardy (Penguin). All the usual Wessex ingredients, from rural lust to the vengeance of the gods, are there. But, unusually for Hardy, the story has a happy ending. Farmer Boldwood, mad for the love of Bathsheba Everdene, kills her husband. True to the Hardy tradition, he is hanged – thus allowing Gabriel Oak to marry his true love.

Brideshead Revisited by Evelyn Waugh (Penguin). Most of the characters are repulsive and all hold views that I despise. But the book is so well written and its ideas so interesting, I find it irresistible. I read it time after time and I always cry when Julia Flyte tells Charles Ryder that she cannot marry him. Waugh has the trick of creating sentiment with a hard edge.

The Old Wives' Tale by Arnold Bennett (Penguin). The greatest of all the Five Town novels is the story of two sisters, one dependable and one flighty, living in the Victorian Potteries with their shopkeeper parents. All the great emotions are there, proving that ordinary people often live extraordinary lives.

The Great Gatsby by F. Scott Fitzgerald (Penguin). Jay Gatsby arrives on Long Island and uses his millions to "build a dream to live by". But Daisy – his lost love – encourages him to believe that she still cares, without considering the consequences of her self-indulgence. The result is catastrophe and one of the most spectacular acts of self-sacrifice in modern literature.

Anglo-Saxon Attitudes by Angus Wilson (Out of print). An archaeological hoax doesn't sound like the stuff of which can't-put-down novels are made. But Wilson makes it the catalyst that changes the lives of all the families it touches. In the end, the loveless hero demonstrates his new-found independence by spending Christmas alone. Thousands of readers must envy and admire his courage.

Denis Healey

The veteran Labour politician Lord Healey now reads poetry rather than modern novels. He discusses the books which have influenced his life in **My Secret Planet***. Here are six of his favourites.*

Issue 192: 20th February 1999

Collected Poems of Emily Dickinson (Running Press). Although she wrote most of her work 150 years ago, hardly anything was published until a century later. Using short lines and everyday words she demonstrated not only an astonishing capacity for expressing her own emotions but also a powerful intellect. Yet she spent the last half of her life as a lonely spinster rarely venturing outside her bedroom in the small town of Amherst in Massachusetts.

War and Peace by Leo Tolstoy (Penguin). In this novel Tolstoy combines a brilliant account of human relations with an understanding of history. It is unique in literature.

Sketches From a Hunter's Album by Ivan Turgenev (Penguin). Although I love all Turgenev's novels, I did not read this collection of short stories until I was over 60, believing it was a Russian Jorrocks' Jaunts and Jollities. In fact it offers the most sensitive and poetic picture of the Russian countryside imaginable, together with the most powerful evocation of morality in The Living Relic.

Collected Poems of W.B. Yeats (Everyman). I find Yeats's poetry an inexhaustible source of pleasure. His later work shows his unique understanding of human beings, not only as individuals but also as political animals.

Wuthering Heights by Emily Brontë (Penguin). I was brought up on the edge of Ilkley Moor looking across Keighley to the home of the Brontë sisters in Howarth. Emily was an outstanding poet, though she is most remembered for Wuthering Heights, which I see as the only Russian novel written in English.

The Brothers Karamazov by Fyodor Dostoevsky (Penguin). The three brothers might have been invented to embody Freud's ego, id and superego. I find Ivan's dream about the Grand Inquisitor the best possible introduction to power politics.

Edward Heath

*Sir Edward Heath, the former prime minister, chooses his six favourite books. His autobiography, **The Course of My Life**, is published by Coronet.*

Issue 220: 4th September 1999

Herbert von Karajan by Richard Osborne (Pimlico). Although nobody could ever question Herbert von Karajan's mastery of the orchestra, he will always remain a controversial figure. This is by far the most impressive biography of him to have appeared to date.

General Theory of Employment, Interest and Money by John Maynard Keynes (Macmillan). I read this book as an undergraduate, when it was first published. These days everyone claims to know all about "Keynesianism", but few seem actually to have read this fascinating, seminal and largely misunderstood work. More should fully digest it.

Racing Skipper by Robin Aisher (Out of print). Like his late father, Owen, whom I always found immensely supportive, Robin Aisher has been a tower of strength in the British sailing fraternity. This is as good an account as I have read of what it's like to sail competitively out on the open sea.

Chequers by Norma Major (HarperCollins). When I was prime minister, I spent as much time as possible at Chequers, the country home provided for all prime ministers. Norma fell in love with the place too, and this excellent book is as affectionate as it is interesting.

Buddenbrooks by Thomas Mann (Minerva). I first read this great masterpiece as a young man. The tale of a family's rise and fall is as poignant as ever. It also retains its infinite possibilities as metaphor and analogy. Not an easy read, but worth the effort.

Churchill – A Life by Martin Gilbert (Tiptree). Sir Martin Gilbert has devoted his life to the study of Sir Winston Churchill, but his thoroughness in no way precludes enjoyment. It is doubtful whether this excellent distillation of a professional life's work can ever be bettered.

Simon Heffer

Journalist Simon Heffer chooses his six favourite memoirs. His biography of Enoch Powell, **Like the Roman: The Life of Enoch Powell**, *is published by Weidenfeld and Nicolson.*

Issue 350: 23rd March 2002

Praeterita by John Ruskin (out of print). From the first, arresting sentence – "I am, and my father was before me, a violent Tory of the old school" – Ruskin illustrates the inseparability of his life from a philosophy that might shock those who imagine, wrongly, that he was a forefather of British socialism. Few books display such breadth of learning and humanity as this.

Recollections of Three Reigns by Sir Frederick Ponsonby (Out of print). Fritz Ponsonby served Queen Victoria, Edward VII and George V and scandalised the court when he published this urbane but Technicolor book of memories of his life near the Throne.

The Missing Will by Michael Wharton (Out of print). The man who was The Telegraph's Peter Simple writes arrestingly of his haphazard journey from obscurity to Fleet Street, via battles with Stalinists at the BBC and a Cumbrian fantasy world.

Enemies of Promise by Cyril Connolly (Andre Deutsch). Connolly's reminiscence of his education forms only a third of this book, the rest of which is a critical survey of literature. Like Waugh, he succeeds in highlighting the formative in-fluences on his creativity, and in depicting the tensions of the world in which he grew up – in his case, Eton after WWI.

Autobiography by John Cowper Powys (Syracuse University). Powys's greatness is only now being appreciated 40 years after his death. His power to see and feel, and his knack of writing a 350,000-word account of his life without mentioning any woman but his mother, make this a remarkable work.

A Little Learning by Evelyn Waugh (Penguin). Waugh's tragicomic account of his early life was the first volume of an autobiography. Sadly, he did not live to complete any further instalments, but this provides a remarkably objective picture of the insecurities and snobbery that forged a great satirical novelist.

91

Zoë Heller

Journalist Zoë Heller chooses her six favourite books.
*Her novel, **Everything You Know**, is published by Viking.*

Issue 208: 12th June 1999

Photo: Sigrid E Strada

I Capture the Castle by Dodie Smith (Virago). An adolescent girl describes life with her Bohemian English family in a ruined castle. Among other things, it's about falling in love for the first time. I read it when I was nine and it was, I think, the first book to make me weep. I enjoy it just as much – and blub just as copiously – when I read it now.

Sport of Nature by Nadine Gordimer (Jonathan Cape). The story of a white South African woman and her conversion to the anti-apartheid struggle. Sounds rather preachy – but it isn't. Gordimer writes about modern women and modern politics better than almost anyone.

Our Mutual Friend by Charles Dickens (Penguin). The last complete novel that Dickens wrote. It has all the usual Dickensian virtues together with an unusually sexy hero. The ironic, witty Eugene Wrayburn, beneath whose cynical exterior beats a feeling heart, was the first fictional character I really fancied.

Herzog by Saul Bellow (Penguin). I like all Saul Bellow's novels, but this one, I like the best. It's about an American academic having – and then recovering from – a late-life crisis. It's pretty much the perfect 20th century novel. It also contains the best description of a character's hair in contemporary fiction.

The Moronic Inferno by Martin Amis (Penguin). A collection of his journalism about America. It's very, very funny and it always makes me want to sit down and start writing. I particularly enjoy his account of visiting a southern Baptist convention, where he is addressed by everybody as "Marty".

Son of the Morning Star by E.H. Carr (Pimlico). Principally, a very detailed account of General Custer's last stand, but also a brilliant, obsessive history of the American West, full of arcane facts about scalping methods and cowboy hygiene.

Carl Hiaasen

*Novelist Carl Hiaasen chooses six books that made him laugh in unexpected ways. His novel, **Skinny Dip**, is published by Bantam Press.*

Issue 485: 6th November 2004

Car by Harry Crews (out of print). A wonderfully demented story set in Florida about a man who eats a car, piece by piece, in order to win a prize. It's a brilliant satire on the decline of American culture, and the commercialisation and the degradation of the spirit to the point that people are prepared to do anything to win a contest.

The Water-Method Man by John Irving (Transworld). A totally original and rather twisted novel. It's about a man with a urinary tract complaint that affects all things in his life, in a way that one would think would be insurmountable. It turns into a very funny novel about life and the obstacles we must endure and overcome.

Riotous Assembly by Tom Sharpe (Arrow). This is a brilliant satire on South African apartheid. The humour and the descriptions of the institutions that he's lampooning are wonderful and remind me of the great American satires. Sharpe makes sure that while you're laughing, you are also pondering the heavier picture.

Slaughter House 5 by Kurt Vonnegut (Vintage). An extraordinarily witty book about a grave and tragic episode in the war. Vonnegut is able to accomplish a balancing act between the satire and the subject matter. His instinct for the humorous line, the dialogue and pace keep this book compelling page after page.

Catch 22 by Joseph Heller (Vintage). This book had a greater effect on me than any other. I was struck by the sheer ambition of writing a hysterically funny novel about something as bleak and depressing as war. For a young writer starting out, not knowing what the limits are, you read this book and realise there are no limits, no rules.

Ninety-two in the Shade by Thomas McGuane (Vintage). Set in the Florida Keys, it's about a feud between two fishing guides. It's epically funny, tragic and illuminating and so true to the Florida where I grew up. McGuane is a writer who will hit you with a sentence that makes your jaw drop.

Christopher Hibbert

Historian Christopher Hibbert, author of **The Rise and Fall of the House of Medici**, chooses six of his favourite books on Italy. His book, **The Marlboroughs – John and Sarah Churchill 1650-1744**, is published by Viking.

Issue 328: 13th October 2001

A History of Venice by John Julius Norwich (Penguin). This is the crowded history of the most beautiful of cities, from its misty beginnings on the islands of Rialto to the days of the last doge. Written with wit, panache and a scholarship lightly worn by the chairman of the Venice in Peril Fund.

The Leopard by Giuseppe di Lampedusa (Harvill Press). This remarkable panoramic historical novel – set in Sicily in the 1860s at the time of the movement for a united Italy, the Risorgimento – is the work of a Sicilian prince who died before it was published. It is a masterly evocation of troubled times and divided loyalties.

Mussolini by Denis Mack Smith (Phoenix). A brilliant and convincing account of the man who was Italy's dictator for more than 20 years and who attracted more admiration than anyone else in the whole course of Italian history.

Pictures from Italy by Charles Dickens (Penguin). Not to be recommended for its facile comments on art and architecture but for its characteristically idiosyncratic sketches of Italian people and their lives in the 1840s. Written when Dickens travelled through Italy with his wife, sister-in-law, five children, two nursemaids, one courier and the family dog.

Garibaldi's Defence of the Roman Republic by G.M. Trevelyan (Phoenix). The first volume of a trilogy of studies of the making of Italy first published in 1907, this is an enduring masterpiece of narrative history and a moving portrait of the great Garibaldi.

Lives of the Artists by Giorgio Vasari (Oxford Paperbacks). The 16th century critic's short, deft and vivid accounts of the Italian masters who lived and worked in Renaissance Florence, from Cimabue and Giotto to Leonardo, Raphael and Michelangelo – whose work alone, said Vasari, "would teach us how to attain perfection in design".

Peter Hitchens

*Peter Hitchens, Daily Express columnist and author of **The Abolition of Britain**, chooses his six favourite thrillers.*

Issue 270: 26th August 2000

Night falls on the City by Sarah Gainham (Out of print).
Set in Vienna before the National Socialist take-over of Austria, an anti-Nazi journalist tries to flee from the Gestapo, but fails to make it across the border. This account of life and survival in a police state leads to some very dark places indeed.

The Night of Wenceslas by Lionel Davidson (Arrow). Buy this funny, unpredictable page-turner about espionage in Prague and you get The Rose of Tibet thrown in for free. This is a good thing, because I can't decide which of the two is the best thriller written since the war. Davidson is unique and should be better known.

Judgement on Deltchev by Eric Ambler (Pan). Scandalously few of Ambler's books are in print. This wry account of the truth behind a Fifties Stalinist show trial was Ambler's farewell to his pre-war communist sympathies.

That Hideous Strength by C.S. Lewis (HarperCollins). A beautiful English university town is taken over by a sinister government department that calls itself the NICE. I have seldom read a more merciless description of the moral cowardice and greed that infect politics. Real, fearsome evil is unleashed as the bulldozers move in to modernise the ancient groves.

In the Wet by Nevil Shute (Out of print). A Labour government determined to destroy the monarchy, an attempt to murder the Queen and an essay on the limits of democracy, all wrapped up in an ingenious time-shift. Why is this clever, fascinating book out of print?

When the Kissing Had to Stop by Constantine Fitz Gibbon (Bellew Publishing). A Fifties fantasy about a Soviet takeover of Britain, following the election of a doddering ban-the-bomb prime minister, set in a decadent and seedy London.

Eric Hobsbawm

The historian Eric Hobsbawm chooses five books which demonstrate the extraordinary merits of photography as an eye on the past.

Issue 160: 4th July 1998

Photo: Jerry Bauer

Workers: An Archaeology of the Industrial Age by Sebastiao Salgado (Phaidon). These photographs offer a visual history of the Industrial Revolution – "a time when men and women at work with their hands provided the central axis of the world". An epic book by an economist who took to the camera.

Citizens of the Twentieth Century: Portrait Photographs 1892-1929 by August Sander (MITP). This formed the basis of an ambitious project to portray "the existing social order" using, essentially, the methods of the provincial family photographer. The result is a work of extraordinary depth and capacity to move.

The Secret Paris of the Thirties by Brassai (Thames & Hudson). Brassai (1899-1984) was a cosmopolitan Hungarian, central to the history of 20th-century photography. In the Paris of the Thirties there was no Toulouse Lautrec around, only a star-struck Hungarian with a camera.

The Decisive Moment: Images à la Sauvette by Henri Cartier Bresson (Simon & Shuster, out of print). Cartier Bresson is probably the greatest and certainly the most influential photographer of the century. Surrealism taught him to let his intuition recognise the "decisive moment"; the pocket camera allowed him to ambush it.

Nadar by Nigel Gosling (Meulenhoff, out of print). Felix Tournachon (known as Nadar, 1820-1910) was the greatest portrait photographer of his century, who captured almost everybody who was anybody in Paris.

Wendy Holden

*Bestselling novelist Wendy Holden picks six books to relax with. Her new novel, **Fame Fatale**, a funny look at the world of PR and journalism, is published by Headline.*

Issue 341: 19th January 2002

Secrets of the Heart by Elizabeth Buchan (Penguin). Elizabeth Buchan is a wonderful writer and I adored her latest book, about a girl who inherits a romantic old house and plenty of problems to go with it. Her characters are beautifully rounded – especially the embittered farmer and the insecure mistress whose chin is beginning to sag. Enchanting.

I am an Oil Tanker by Fi Glover (Ebury). I'm a huge fan of Fi Glover's Radio Five Live show and this book is brilliant – a hilarious account of her travels round the world investigating weird and wonderful radio stations. Sort of Bill Bryson but better-looking, and with a radio dial.

Between Males by Fiona Walker (Hodder & Stoughton). A hilarious account of what happens when career girl Odette decides to follow her heart and open a restaurant. I particularly loved the amusing pastiches of contemporary kitchen culture – celebrity chefs, wine bars that look like operating theatres etc. Great stuff.

Out of the Blue by Isabel Woolf (HarperCollins). I love writing ghastly characters in my own books, but struggle with the good ones. Here, in this touching, funny tale of a thirtysomething marriage breakdown, Woolf has pulled off a great feat – a heroine as hilarious as she is nice.

The Daisy Chain by Alexandra Campbell (Penguin). Alexandra Campbell is a razor-sharp commentator on modern life and aspirations. Her latest novel – about the way first love never dies – is great. It's also probably one of the first romantic novels ever about burglary.

Madame Bovary by Gustave Flaubert (Penguin Popular Classics). Expecting tragedy – which of course I got – I was surprised and delighted by the amount of comedy in Flaubert's book, mostly at the expense of the aspirational middle classes. As a connoisseur of social climbers (all my books feature ghastly ones), this was a great treat.

James Holland

*James Holland, historian and author of the bestselling **Fortress Malta: An Island Under Siege 1942-1943**, chooses his six favourite war books. His novel, **The Burning Blue**, is published by William Heinemann.*

Issue 449: 28th February 2004

Sword of Honour by Evelyn Waugh (Penguin). Waugh is my favourite author and this trilogy contains some of the best novels to have emerged from the Second World War. Guy Crouchback is a brilliant creation: the ultimate ordinary man trying to make sense of extraordinary events. Hilarious, tragic, and incredibly moving.

The English Patient by Michael Ondaatje (Picador). This book contains some of the most lyrical, lingering prose I have ever read. The seductiveness of wartime North Africa and Italy is brilliantly depicted. Romantic and haunting, it is a novel I have returned to time and again.

First Light by Geoffrey Wellum (Penguin). I was lucky to read this before it reached any publisher and am not remotely surprised at its subsequent success. I've read many Battle of Britain books, but this stands above even The Last Enemy as the best flying memoir ever written.

A Sailor's Odyssey by Viscount Cunningham (Out of print). Cut from the same cloth as Nelson, Cunningham was bullish, inspirational and happiest when in the thick of action. This wonderful autobiography is full of humour, daring and adventure and is one of the best histories of the Royal Navy in the first half of the last century.

The Recollections of Rifleman Bowlby by Alex Bowlby (Cassell). Bowlby served in the Rifle Brigade in northern Italy. He wrote this memoir 25 years after the fighting ended. Few accounts have portrayed the gruelling reality of war so vividly.

The Second World War by Winston S. Churchill (Out of print). These six volumes make for fascinating and entertaining reading. A history of the War as seen through the eyes of our wartime leader. Full of memos' and missives sent and received by Churchill, it is great to read in chunks or to dip into.

Michael Holroyd

*The biographer Michael Holroyd has written lives of Lytton Strachey, Augustus John and Bernard Shaw, as well as his autobiography, **Basil Street Blues**. Here he selects six successful experiments in biography.*

Issue 174: 10th October 1998

My Relations with Carlyle by James Anthony Froude (Out of print). This lucid and poignant account shows how Froude's health and happiness were ruined by trying to write a truthful biography in the 19th century, under what Carlyle himself called a "Damocles Sword of respectability".

Footsteps: Adventures of a Romantic Biographer by Richard Holmes (Flamingo). An influential book that blends autobiography, travelogue and adventure story. Holmes takes the lives of four diverse writers – R.L. Stevenson, Mary Wollstonecraft, Shelley and the tragic Gérard de Nerval – and follows them in a narrative of charm and originality.

The Quest for Corvo: An Experiment in Biography by A.J.A. Symons (Quartet). This is a genuinely innovative biography, brilliantly tracing Symons's pursuit of the elusive and irascible "Baron Corvo", alias the novelist Frederick Rolfe. A fascinating piece of detective work.

Portrait of a Marriage by Nigel Nicolson (Phoenix). Nicolson interleaves his mother Vita Sackville-West's posthumous autobiography with his own biographical enquiry to uncover the truth of his parents' unconventional marriage. This courageous experiment has established itself as a modern classic.

In Search of J.D. Salinger by Ian Hamilton (Bloomsbury). Hamilton set out to write a conventional biography of his invisible subject. Confronted by Salinger's implacable hostility, he turned a setback to artful advantage with a spellbinding story of the chase.

Brief Lives by John Aubrey (Boydell). These spontaneous impressions owe more to Aubrey's imaginative faculty than to pedestrian research. His exotic glimpses into 16th- and 17th-century life provide vivid examples of the scholarly value of gossip.

Douglas Hurd

*Former Conservative foreign secretary Douglas Hurd chooses his six favourite books. His own books include **The Shape of Ice** and **Ten Minutes to Turn the Devil**, both published by Little, Brown.*

Issue 250: 8th April 2000

The Forsyte Saga by John Galsworthy (Penguin). The thoughts and habits of upper-middle-class London are brilliantly portrayed through the reigns of Victoria, Edward and George. Soames Forsyte begins as a humourless prig, but manages to capture his author's sympathy before his sudden death.

The Collected Poems of Philip Larkin (Faber). Savage language, behind which lurk compassion and a strange conservative radicalism. Larkin despised modern intellectual fashion. He understood Remembrance Day, churchgoing, the Empire and the English countryside, while describing their downfall.

Full Moon by P.G. Wodehouse (Penguin). Written both in his best period, 1947, and in his best setting, Blandings Castle. This novel shows Wodehouse's complete mastery of language and plot. Requires to be savoured slowly, preferably read aloud.

Decline and Fall by Evelyn Waugh (Penguin). The story rushes full cycle from the drunken Bullingdon Club baying for broken glass, through an immortal Welsh prep school, to a stylish marriage for the anti-hero, his imprisonment and return to Oxford. The characters, although not credible, are unforgettable.

The Last Chronicle of Barset by Anthony Trollope (Penguin). The proud, threadbare Reverend Crawley is accused of stealing a cheque. Mrs Proudit dies just when she seemed immortal. Not his best-known novel, but perhaps his best; mixes real feeling with gentle Barsetshire satire.

There are plenty of good biographies of Queen Victoria, that amazing, troublesome, but in the end sympathetic sovereign. I favour (better than Lytton Strachey) **Queen Victoria** by Giles St Aubyn (Out of print).

Bernard Ingham

*Bernard Ingham, journalist, author and former No.10 press secretary, chooses six of his favourite books. His memoir, **The Wages of Spin**, is published by John Murray.*

Issue 405: 19th April 2003

The Call of the Wild by Jack London (Puffin). My father gave me a copy of this classic, still covered in brown paper, when I was a boy, perhaps to teach me about nature and all its cruelties and the bond between man and dog. He said I would find it "hard" – in other words, it would make me cry. It did.

Testament of Youth by Vera Brittain (Virago). Nothing I have read about World War I has moved me so intensely as this heart-rendingly personal record by a truly tragic girl (who became Baroness Shirley Williams's mother) of a generation of young men being killed all around her.

The Citadel by A.J. Cronin (Longman). I acquired my copy as a 15-year-old and remember being utterly absorbed by a young doctor's life in the Welsh valleys of the Twenties for a whole Saturday, with a break only to play football for Thistlebottom AFC.

Wuthering Heights by Emily Brontë (Penguin). I choose it not because the late Jean Rook called me a cross between Heathcliff and a pit bull terrier, but because it is an astounding book by an astounding member of an astounding family, set in my native moors.

Nineteen Eighty-Four by George Orwell (Penguin). Communism may have collapsed, but it has been followed by the age of the spin doctor. This makes George Orwell essential and compelling reading – and, sadly, only too relevant.

The Last Letter Home by Vilhelm Moberg (Warner). The last of this Swedish writer's tremendous quartet of books about the Swedish emigration to America and the making of a new land. It is often heroic and achingly sad.

Richard Ingrams

*Richard Ingrams, editor of The Oldie, author and columnist, chooses his favourite books about ruffians and rogues. His biography, **The Life and Adventures of William Cobbett**, is published by HarperCollins.*

Issue 530: 24th September 2005

Mary Archer by Margaret Crick (Simon & Schuster). It is impossible to disentangle Mary Archer's life from that of her husband Jeffrey. He has been described as a loveable rogue, but there's nothing very loveable about either of them. It is fascinating to read how prim and proper Mary ended up like Jeffrey – ruthless and manipulative.

The Gamblers by John Pearson (Arrow Books). Gripping account of gamblers at the Clermont Club in the Sixties. One, James Goldsmith, became hugely rich, and with it, egotistical, power-mad and deeply unpleasant. Death – murder and suicide – is the leitmotif of a bizarre tale.

The Fall of Conrad Black by Jacquie McNish and Sinclair Stewart (Penguin). A thriller tracing the downward path of The Daily Telegraph's former owner, the pompous Conrad Black, and his glitzy moll, journalist Barbara Amiel. A satisfying tale of arrogance and greed brought low.

Bare-Faced Messiah: The True Story of L. Ron Hubbard by Russell Miller (Out of print). The story of the founder of the Church of Scientology, which attracts adherents the world over, including Hollywood stars. Revered by his followers as a mystic and war hero, Hubbard was a con-man who ended his life on the run from the FBI.

Fayed by Tom Bower (Pan Macmillan). The life of the notorious Egyptian retailer is chronicled in ruthless detail. Branded by the DTI as a liar, guilty of deception on a grand scale, Fayed is still with us, still insisting that Diana and his son Dodi were victims of a Royal conspiracy.

Alastair Campbell by Peter Oborne and Simon Walters (Aurum Press). This is the story of a tabloid journalist who rose to become "the second most powerful man in Britain". Becoming more and more autocratic and aggressive, Campbell engineered his own downfall when he insisted on pursuing the MoD scientist Dr David Kelly.

Virginia Ironside

*Virginia Ironside, agony aunt for The Independent and the Sunday Mirror and author, chooses her six favourite books. Her book, **You'll Get Over It – the Rage of Bereavement**, is published by Penguin.*

Issue 190: 6th February 1999

Twenty Thousand Streets Under the Sky by Patrick Hamilton (Vintage). If Delafield was the original Bridget Jones, Hamilton was the original Jeffrey Bernard, writing about Soho in the Thirties. His beautifully written books are peopled with creepy salesmen in balding camel-hair coats and con-artists blundering through the fog to the pub.

Memoirs of the Forties by Julian Maclaren-Ross (Penguin, out of print). More lowlife in Soho. Maclaren-Ross was a familiar figure in Fitzrovia with his silver-topped cane. He writes brilliantly about wartime London, with marvellous portraits of people like Dylan Thomas and Graham Greene.

At Mrs Lippincote's by Elizabeth Taylor (Virago). Published just after the war, this is an agonising Ayckbournian account of married life in suburbia. I love all her books because they remind me of my own childhood visits to middle-class relations in Esher and Weybridge.

The Man in the Moon by Andrew Barrow (Mandarin). William, a lonely young man who thinks he's a comic genius, lodges in Chelsea in the Sixties. During the day he goes to the office. That's about it. The book, however, is extraordinary, and Barrow's ear for conversation superb.

Prater Violet by Christopher Isherwood (Mandarin). Yes, another book set in Thirties London. It's about Isherwood's relationship with Viennese film director Friedrich Bergmann as they work on a romantic film together. A moving, spiritual last couple of pages make this an extraordinary little gem.

The Diary of a Provincial Lady by E.M. Delafield (Virago). Delafield was the Bridget Jones of her era – only she wasn't a singleton, but married with two children. A painfully funny look at life in a Devon village between the wars.

Lucy Irvine

*Lucy Irvine, who has survived two year-long stints on tropical islands, chooses her six favourite books. **Faraway**, her account of her experiences on Pigeon Island, is published by Corgi.*

Issue 316: 21st July 2001

Falling by Colin Thubron (Penguin). A jewel of a novel in which a young man falls for a trapeze artiste who lives for the perfect swallow-dive. Wobbled one night by their relationship, she breaks her back, falling. Seeing no desire in her to live paralysed, he switches off her life-support system and is imprisoned. But being Thubron, it's handled subtly, and interwoven with the theme of The Fall of Man.

Lord Of The Flies by William Golding (Faber & Faber). An outstanding piece of polished literature, it's not only a terrific story for teenagers but should be reread by every book-loving adult for its sheer lyricism – as well as the dark symbolism.

Foe by J.M. Coetzee (Penguin). I've examined numerous reworkings of the Selkirk/Crusoe tale but this one's stuck. Written from the angle of a woman washed up on Crusoe's island, Coetzee follows what happens when – Crusoe having died – his heroine seeks out Defoe in London, with a tongueless Friday, to sell their tale.

A Biography Of Lawrence Durrell by Ian MacNiven (Faber & Faber). For all who've been through a Durrell phase, this is riveting. What drove the man? Who's who out of real life in The Alexandria Quartet and how did Larry manage, or mismanage, his numerous affairs? Read and be captivated.

The Plague by Albert Camus (Penguin). I've read this three times and each time been appalled and enthralled by its acuity on internal and external "exile" – Camus's speciality. A story about a town isolated by sickness, the implications about humanity's survival-urge go deep.

At The Jerusalem by Paul Bailey (Bloomsbury). This superficially simple novel about an elderly lady moving into a Home is an intricately wrought portrayal of the agony experienced by the infliction of subtle indignities. Bailey uses dialogue and inner thought to marvellous effect.

Glenda Jackson

Glenda Jackson, MP for Hampstead and Highgate and past London mayoral candidate, chooses her six favourite books.

Issue 241: 5th February 2000

Little Women by Louisa M. Alcott (Penguin). One of the first books I read as a girl and later recorded as a talking book. Although set in the American Civil War, the story is relevant today. The March girls are very believable and as a group encompass the range of female archetypes. The mother, struggling to keep her fierce temper in check, is particularly recognisable.

The Great Gatsby by F. Scott Fitzgerald (Penguin). This is one of the most perfect novels I have ever read. It is the story of the shady, mysterious financier Jay Gatsby's destructive passion for Daisy Buchanan. Although he is almost anonymous, you learn much about him and the world he inhabits.

The Secret Garden by Frances Hodgson Burnett (Penguin). Another children's story that I read as a talking book. The transformation of a spoilt, ratty little girl into somebody that everyone eventually likes is quite fascinating. The heroine grows and blossoms as the garden she discovers and restores comes to life.

Persuasion by Jane Austen (Penguin). I constantly reread all Austen's works. I rediscovered Persuasion when I was on holiday and it was the only book in English in the local shop. I hadn't read it for ten years – since I'd been forced to at school – and found I couldn't put it down for two days. I regret ever closing the door on Austen.

Possession by Emily Dickinson. This long poem is found in The Selected Poems of Emily Dickinson (Bloomsbury Press). Dickinson is a particular heroine of mine. She manages to bring infinite variety to her work, although she had a limited experience of the outside world – she remained single and after her twenties rarely left Amherst, MA.

Gaudy Nights by Dorothy L. Sayers (Hodder). Lord Peter Wimsey's adventure in which Sayers creates a vivid picture of an Oxford women's college between the wars. Harriet finally accepts Wimsey's proposal. It's a little dated, but still a terrific read.

P.D. James

The author P.D. James chooses her six favourite detective stories – "golden oldies, all of which I can re-read with pleasure". Her autobiography, **Time to be Earnest***, is published by Faber.*

Issue 228: 30th October 1999

The Tiger in the Smoke by Margery Allingham (Penguin). This tale, largely set in a London fog, refutes the criticism that the detective story can't accurately deal with the absolutes of good and evil. In its evocation of atmosphere and its portrayal of the two main contrasting characters, it is a masterpiece of the genre.

The Murder of Roger Ackroyd by Agatha Christie (HarperCollins). Christie is not my favourite detective writer, but it would be perverse not to include this tour de force of a novel. The solution is sometimes seen as unfair, but no one could deny its originality, nor complain that the clues are not there for those with eyes to see them.

The Franchise Affair by Josephine Tey (Penguin). This is a true detective story, but one without a murder. A teenager accuses two respectable women of virtual slavery. Her tale is persuasive, but is it true? A lawyer sets out to vindicate the women. The mystery is intriguing but the power of the book lies in the characterisation of the three main figures.

The Hound of the Baskervilles by Arthur Conan Doyle (Penguin). This shiver-inducing book is not without errors, but the story of the terrifying hound, together with Doyle's narrative power, ensure that this novel retains a hold on our imaginations.

The Moonstone by Wilkie Collins (Penguin). T.S. Eliot described this book as "the first, the longest and the best of modern English detective stories". The tale adumbrates most of the later conventions of detective fiction and introduces Sgt Cuff, one of the greatest eccentric detectives. The story is not the first detective story, but it is the most distinguished.

The Nine Tailors by Dorothy L. Sayers (Coronet). Sayers helped lift the detective story from mere puzzle to serious fiction. The setting is the vanished world of the East Anglian fens and she makes masterly use of its bleak isolation.

Sir Anthony Jay

Sir Anthony Jay, co-writer of Yes, Minister, has also published **How to Beat Sir Humphrey.** *Here he selects six books he considers essential reading for new ministers.*

Issue 105: 7th June 1997

Your Disobedient Servant by Leslie Chapman (Out of print).
There has never been such a devastating account of civil service extravagance, waste, obstruction and concealment written by such a senior, lifelong civil servant. A treasure-trove of horrifying incidents, none of which was ever denied.

The Diaries of a Cabinet Minister by Richard Crossman (Mandarin). The first of the three volumes is best for new ministers. He describes his rapid climb up the ministerial learning curve, and his collisions and collusions with his aptly named permanent secretary, Dame Evelyn Sharp.

Inside Number 10 by Marcia Williams (Out of print).
Excellent account of Labour moving in after 13 years of Conservative government, with acute insights into relationships between ministers and civil servants.

The View From No. 11 by Nigel Lawson (Transworld). Every minister must understand how the Treasury works and thinks. This is the definitive work, with far more information and far less self-vindication than most ministerial memoirs.

Diaries by Alan Clark (Orion). The real sensation of this wonderful book is the truth and honesty that shine through every entry. My only regret is that it was not published while we were still writing Yes, Minister.

Whitehall by Peter Hennessy (Fontana). The classic guide to the structure, history and culture of the great departments of state, not omitting the personalities, the rows and the anecdotes. An excellent read.

Simon Jenkins

*Simon Jenkins, the author and columnist, chooses his favourite books with a topographical theme. His book, **England's Thousand Best Houses**, is published by Penguin.*

Issue 493: 8th January 2005

Pickwick Papers by Charles Dickens (Penguin). Dickens brought London to life through the antics of Pickwick and his friends. Here was town and country, passion, humour and suspense. To crown all was the Christmas party which fixed that ceremony in the liturgy of Britishness ever since.

People and Places by James Lees-Milne (John Murray). I doubt anyone did more to romanticise and thus save the great houses of Britain. These are tragicomic tales of aristocrats in distress, as Lees-Milne gently lifted from them their ancestral birthrights and deposited them in our most genteel nationalised industry.

The World 1950-2000 by Jan Morris (Faber). Morris's collected travel essays leave no stone uncoloured and no anecdote unrelated. To visit with her is to have another eye and another ear. In Venice, Morris remains supreme: what Ruskin offered the mind she offers the senses.

English Parish Churches as Works of Art by Alex Clifton-Taylor (Out of print). Clifton-Taylor conjured churches from the earth and stone from which they came. He watched them form into patterns, moulded by the hands of men into glories of vernacular art. He revealed the church for Everyman and made me love these places.

Pallas Guides by Peter Sager (Pallas Athene). After Morton, Pevsner and Shell, where to turn for new writing about Britain? Pallas, led by Peter Sager. Information is interspersed with historical asides. Perhaps, like Pevsner, it takes a German to detect the true character of Britain.

London in the 20th century by Jerry White (Out of print). London's topographical corpse has been dissected a thousand times, yet its darkest ages remain little recorded. Here, White sweeps through a London where historians still fear to tread: the modern city. If you want to know why London is the triumphant mess of today, White's the man.

John Keegan

John Keegan, the military historian, chooses his six favourite books.
*His book, **The First World War**, is published by Hutchinson*

Issue 187: 16th January 1999

Swallows and Amazons by Arthur Ransome (Red Fox) was the first proper book I read, aged seven. It completely enthralled me, carrying me from look-and-say to full-blown literature in one jump. Re-reading it recently I see why. Wonderful story, beautifully written.

Kim by Rudyard Kipling (Penguin). Kipling makes one believe in genius. Every single quality of the great writer leaps from the page – unforgettable characterisation, unrelenting pace of narrative, extraordinary evocation of atmosphere, deep moral sense. No wonder Indians love it as much as the English.

The Habsburg Empire by C.A. Macartney (Weidenfeld & Nicholson, out of print). A history book for historians. Macartney learnt about the most complex of European empires as a diplomat. As a fellow of All Souls, he turned his knowledge into a literary treasure-house of arcane information and brilliant insights.

Sword of Honour by Evelyn Waugh (Penguin). Waugh's derided snobbishness results in a flawless portrait of that central, national institution – the British army. Toffs, thugs, trimmers, traitors are all there, as well as a vital slice of mid-20th-century history.

The Thirty-Nine Steps by John Buchan (Penguin). The plot is nonsensical and the characters are cardboard. Its sublime certainty of what is right and wrong makes it nevertheless the supreme spy story, thanks to Buchan's brilliant style and literary self-confidence.

The Struggle for Europe by Chester Wilmot (Wordsworth Editions). The book that taught me how to write military history. Wilmot's ability to combine strategic analysis with eye-witness accounts of the experience of battle sets a standard that all military historians have to match.

Marian Keyes

The author Marian Keyes chooses her six favourite books.
*Her novel, **The Other Side of the Story**, is published by Penguin.*

Issue 465: 19th June 2004

The Third Policeman by Flann O'Brien (HarperCollins). A masterpiece of language and imagination which was only published posthumously. Subversive, wildly inventive language leads us into a compelling kaleidoscope of netherworlds, until the shocking denouement on the last page when suddenly everything makes sense.

Three Blind Mice by Caron Freeborn (Little Brown).
This haunting story of belonging, power, ambition and loss stands outside most obvious genres. It's part thriller – "East End noir" – and part dark, erotic love story.
A debut novel, written with verve and confidence, it stayed with me long after I'd finished it.

Lorelei's Secret by Carolyn Parkhurst (Sceptre). Paul's wife Lexy has died – but was it an accident or suicide? The only witness was her dog, the Lorelei of the title, and desperate for knowledge, Paul decides to teach Lorelei to speak. Nothing like as whimsical as it sounds, this is a charming, tender study in grief.

Don't Let's Go to the Dogs Tonight by Alexandra Fuller (Picador).
A gloriously evocative memoir of Fuller's African childhood during the Seventies and Eighties. She presents painful (and painfully funny) family tragedy while being part of a white farming community in the midst of Black African independence.

Feeling Sorry for Celia by Jaclyn Moriarty (Pan Macmillan).
This hilarious novel appeals across the board. Eschewing traditional narrative, the story unfolds via diary entries, letters and memos. In fact, the relationship between teenage Elisabeth and her mother is revealed entirely through notes they leave for each other on the fridge. Literary Prozac.

The Secret World of the Irish Male by Joseph O'Connor (Out of print). A collection of comic journalism from the author of Star of the Sea. Side-splittingly, achingly funny from the very first line. Still makes me weep with laughter no matter how many times I read it.

Mary Killen

*Author, journalist and Spectator agony aunt Mary Killen chooses her six favourite books. Her book, **Dear Mary... Your Social Dilemmas Resolved**, is published by Constable.*

Issue 237: 8th January 2000

A La Recherche de Temps Perdu by Marcel Proust, translated by C.K. Scott Moncrieff (Vintage). Proust "gives you another life", said John Gross, who gave me volume one during a low point of my own. Proust also shows you that the brain really is a muscle whose performance can be enhanced through exercise as the contents of the lengthy sentences become progressively easier to assimilate.

The Life of Doctor Johnson by James Boswell (Wordsworth). The combined value of two brilliant men. Of all writing styles I most envy Boswell's. "Mrs Johnson had a bosom of more than ordinary protuberance," for example.

The Pursuit of Love by Nancy Mitford (Penguin). It gives laughter, romance, the pleasures of snobbery and also cosiness. The reader feels embosomed by the glamorous Radlett family and the action generally takes place in comfortable rooms. Linda Radlett is lovely and Fabrice a credible love object.

Gossip by Andrew Barrow (Out of print). In 1978, Andrew Barrow, now a novelist, used gossip as a vehicle for satire. Combing the Colindale Newspaper Library he compiled a history of the years 1900-70 as seen through more trivial news items. Some readers miss the point. The humour is cumulative.

Le Grand Meaulnes by Henri Alain-Fournier (Penguin). Everything that is beautiful about adolescence is here. So is the sense of being just within grasp of a perfect world – glimpsed, now out of reach. On Sunday afternoons the narrator's father goes fishing "sur la bord de quelque étang couvert de brume". The phrase conjures up vividly my own dank adolescence in Northern Ireland.

Just William by Richmal Crompton (Macmillan). Any book in the series gives me happiness and makes me laugh.

Miles Kington

The Independent columnist and humourist Miles Kington chooses six of his favourite books

Issue 366: 13th July 2002

Best of Myles by Myles na Gopaleen (Flamingo). Selected columns by Flann O'Brien's other nom-de-guerre. Who is the funniest columnist ever? I used to go for S.J. Perelman, then for Beachcomber, and later for Alphonse Allais, but this is the man I come back to each time. Well, this time, anyway.

The Collected Brigadier Gerard Stories by Arthur Conan Doyle (Canongate). Not as good as Sherlock Holmes (what is?), but more undiscovered. These historical yarns, seen through the eyes of a vainglorious Napoleonic officer, are fresh, funny and thrilling. My great-uncle had a collection of 1,000 books on Napoleon. I only had this one. I think I had the better deal.

A Choice of Days: Essays from Happy Days, Newspaper Days, and Heathen Days by H.L. Mencken (Out of print). A great American memoir by the journalist who castigated Prohibition and all other follies of Twenties America, and was also present at the only recorded attempt to play all Beethoven's symphonies in one sitting. Wonderfully serious, wonderfully funny.

Just William's Luck by Richmal Crompton (Macmillan). I still think that William is the funniest rebel-hero ever created. This, as far as I know, is the only full-length William novel Crompton ever wrote. It's wonderful. Some of William's tortuous trains of thought are ahead of Stoppard's.

Voyage en Espagne by Theophile Gautier (Out of print). Young Frenchman goes through Spain in the 1830s. Best travel book I have ever read. Funny, exotic, wild, full of bullfights and ladies, highwaymen and history. John Hatt once asked me what travel book I would like his Eland Books to publish. This one, I said; alas, it's never been translated. Then translate it for me, he said, and I still mean to.

Through the Looking Glass and What Alice Found There by Lewis Carroll (Bloomsbury). Best book about chess ever written.

Robert Lacey

Biographer and historian Robert Lacey selects his five favourite history books. His **Great Tales from English History: Chaucer to the Glorious Revolution** *is published by Little, Brown.*

Issue 489: 4th December 2004

Our Island Story by H.E. Marshall (Out of print). My mother found this gem in W.H. Smith while queuing for the cod liver oil ration – and I was hooked on history for life. Marshall was a redoubtable Scottish governess who turned bedtime stories into Edwardian bestsellers. Long out of print, you can read this on www.digital.library.upenn.edu /books/

In Search of England by Michael Wood (Penguin). Here is original research plus marvellous musing on the Norman Yoke, the legends of Arthur and Robin Hood, and the Lost Life of King Athelstan. History's gaps and fragments, Wood demonstrates, contain truths to rival the facts.

Ecclesiastical History of the English People by Bede (Penguin). Our first English historian, the "Venomous Bede" – as he featured in 1066 and All That – was an expert on the tides, a lover of pepper and had a wry touch when it came to theology. Of King Saul's two wives, he wrote: "How can I comment on this, who have not even been married to one?"

War and Peace by Leo Tolstoy (Penguin). It would be wonderful if conventional history was packed with this much passion and pain. Most historical novels overdo it, but Tolstoy succeeds through restraint – and real knowledge of what battle was about. He was a gunner at Sebastopol, and one of his earliest published stories described a military manoeuvre against those fierce, perennially anti-Russian warriors, the Chechens.

The Making of English Law: King Alfred to the Twelfth Century by Patrick Wormald (Blackwell). Just half of a masterwork by the brilliant medievalist who helped to redefine our understanding of Anglo-Saxon England. Let us hope that Patrick's second volume, near completion at the time of his death earlier this year, sees the light of day.

Lucinda Lambton

*Lucinda Lambton, the writer and television presenter, chooses her six favourite children's books. She has written an introduction to **The House of Tekelden**, by Denys Dawnay (1945), published by Bloomsbury.*

Issue 538: 19th November 2005

The House of Tekelden by Denys Dawnay: (Bloomsbury). As curious as it is clever. This is an artistic and historical parody, written and painted about generations of a family as represented by the great masters of their day; with the twist in the "tail" that they are all dachshunds.

Ozma of Oz along with Frank Baum's 14 other books on Oz (Dover reprints). Every one has a delicate strangeness that was crassly vulgarised on film. Oddities abound, such as Princess Langwidere, who had a choice of 30 heads to put on each morning: "all being of exceeding loveliness, with noses that were Grecian, Roman, retroussé and Oriental".

A Little Princess: The Story of Sarah Crewe by Frances Hodgson Burnett (Penguin). An unabashedly sentimental 19th century story of good triumphing over evil. A saintly, imaginative and wildly rich child is reduced to poverty; then, through marvellous and exotic circumstances, recovers all.

Rupert Bear - any annual from 1936; all extraordinary (Out of print). Set in idyllic English countryside, Rupert and pals sally forth on mind-blasting adventures. First appearing in the Daily Express in 1920, he is still on the go today. During the war, Lord Beaverbrook retained Rupert to lift the nation's morale.

Petland Revisited by The Rev J.G. Wood (Out of print). A grown-up's book, but one that always gripped me as a child; reading of such creatures as Slut the famous pointer pig, who "has been known to point out partridges, pheasants, snipe and rabbits but who would never notice hares".

The Fox's Frolic, Or A Day With The Topsy Turvy Hunt by Sir Francis Burnand (Out of print). Whipcrackingly witty illustrations by Harry B. Neilson of foxes on hounds hunting a "peasant". The elegant heroine sits side-saddle on her rearing mount: "Miss Reynard la belle has a perfect seat / Well-fitting foxgloves and habit neat."

Peter Lamont

Dr Peter Lamont, magician, historian, and author of The Rise of the Indian Rope Trick, chooses his six favourite books on magic. His book, **The First Psychic**, *is published by Little, Brown.*

Issue 537: 12th November 2005

Confessions of a Psychic by Uriah Fuller (Out of print). There are far too many books on how to do tricks, and far too few on why to bother. One way to make magic matter to people is to claim it is real, the result of psychic (or extraordinary psychological) abilities. Martin Gardner, writing as Fuller, provides an imaginative exposé, which illustrates how different such performances can be.

Frame Analysis by Erving Goffman (Out of print). This brilliant treatise on how we see things, and how we can re-frame them, is more insightful than any psychology textbook. A remarkable lesson in observation and deception.

True and False: Heresy and Common Sense for the Actor by David Mamet (Faber & Faber). Robert-Houdin, the father of modern magic, described a conjuror as an actor playing the part of a magician. In this stimulating polemic against Stanislavsky's "method", and in defence of the script, Mamet argues for performance without pretension, in order to provide a more convincing illusion.

Myths To Live By by Joseph Campbell (Souvenir Press). An astonishing collection of essays on the power and value of myth, a book that instils mystery, provokes wonder and suggests the extraordinariness of the lives we lead.

Learned Pigs and Fireproof Women by Ricky Jay (Farrar Strauss & Giroux Inc.). A book of genuine wonders, written with wit, scholarship and a rare understanding of why the weird is not only widespread but also essential to our world.

A Universal History Of Iniquity by Jorge Luis Borges (Out of print). Wonderfully quirky tales of deception and credulity, of wizards and prophets, which walk the line between history and fiction, leaving us to decide whether they are reality or illusion, and whether that matters.

Christopher Lee

The actor Christopher Lee chooses his six favourite books. His autobiography, **Lord of Misrule***, is published by Orion.*

Issue 434: 8th November 2003

Heaven & Hell to Play With by Preston Neal Jones (Limelight Editions USA) This is the story of the making of The Night of the Hunter, which in my opinion is the greatest film ever made, as told by all the people involved in making it. A must-read for all film makers and students of the cinema.

The Light's on at Signpost by George MacDonald Fraser (HarperCollins) What is extraordinary about this book is its devastatingly accurate description of problems that beset our country – particularly with regard to discipline, ideals, manners, punishment and society in general.

Ten Composers by Neville Cardus (Out of print) This is a wonderful book, and I have never read such an insight and appreciation of the great musicians concerned. The author's knowledge of music and musicians is unparalleled.

Stalin: The Court of the Red Tsar by Simon Sebag Montefiore (Weidenfeld & Nicholson) I couldn't put this book down. It's not just the story of the revolutionary and head of the government, but also a fascinating look at Stalin's private life – the man, the father, the husband – and at the private lives of those at his court.

What Just Happened? by Art Linson (Bloomsbury) I have just started reading this. It really is the most revealing and accurate description of what actually goes on behind the scenes in the film industry, and illustrates what a truly remarkable achievement it is ever to get a film made!

Stalingrad by Antony Beevor (Penguin) This is without doubt the most powerful and realistic book I've read about the horrors of war and of the most titanic battle of the Second World War. If the city had fallen, the Germans would probably have conquered the Soviet Union.

Prue Leith

*Prue Leith, the cookery writer and restaurateur, is also the author of the novel, **Leaving Patrick**, a love story published this week by Penguin. Here she chooses her six favourite novels about love.*

Issue 215: 31st July 1999

Birdsong by Sebastian Faulks (Vintage). I hate war novels and read this one only because everyone kept telling me how wonderful it was. They were right. It is a love story set in World War I. It manages to be unputdownable, haunting, sad and uplifting all at once. Contains another great bedroom scene: explicit but still magical.

Cold Mountain by Charles Frazier (Hodder). This recent bestseller deserved all its acclaim. An epic tale of the American Civil War, a soldier's desertion and long trek home to the cold moun-tain of the title – and of his quest for love and sanctuary. You long for, indeed you pray for, a happy ending.

Anna Karenina by Leo Tolstoy (Penguin). Glamorous, flawed Vronsky draws Anna into a doomed affair with tragic consequences. The best-told love story of all time. I defy any reader not to be reduced to tears by the end of the book. Unhappy endings, I fear, can only be handled by truly great writers.

Pride and Prejudice by Jane Austen (Penguin). No one has ever done it better. The Bennet family is delicious, Darcy is drop-dead gorgeous and Mr Collins still makes my flesh creep after umpteen readings. The book will always outshine its TV adaptations.

Barchester Towers by Anthony Trollope (Oxford University Press). Only incidentally a love story although Trollope always sees the girls get their men. But Trollope's women are acutely observed and made of flesh and blood, none more so than the terrifying Bishop's wife, Mrs Proudie.

Private Altars by Katherine Mosby (Out of print). Debut novel by a poet. Totally absorbing Deep South story of a cultivated woman abandoned by her husband in a world of small-town prejudice. Contains the most lyrical sex scene ever.

Penelope Lively

Penelope Lively chooses six books that she constantly revisits. Her collection of short stories, **Beyond the Blue Mountains**, *is in paperback and her novel Spiderweb is published by Viking.*

Issue 140: 14th February 1998

The Iliad and The Odyssey by Homer (Penguin). Andrew Lang's re-tellings of Greek mythology fired me as a child and introduced me to the concept of narrative. As I grew up I realised that the stories are threaded through literature and art. Now I often revisit the mythologies to try to recover that first thrill.

Alice's Adventures in Wonderland and Through the Looking-Glass by Lewis Caroll (Everyman). Again, these were childhood favourites but I go back to them with adult perception to enjoy the brilliant combination of wit, linguistic play and the unique anarchic child's-eye view.

The Diaries of Virginia Woolf (Penguin) are for late-night reading – for a dip into her vivid, immediate world that is entirely alien at first but becomes seductively familiar through her knack for pinning down people and events in flights of hectic language.

Ford Madox Ford's The Good Soldier (Penguin) is one of those novels that stretches the potential of the form to its limits. I re-read it to admire the subtlety of a construction that leaves the reader constantly wrong-footed in assumptions of what has happened and why.

Henry James's What Maisie Knew (Penguin) is again a novel that is different at each reading as you appreciate yet another level of its cleverness – a story of adult depravity seen through the eyes of a child not realising what it is she sees.

Dombey and Son (Penguin) is simply my favourite Dickens. I go back to it for a Dickens fix – to immerse myself in the great London descriptions and the ornate characters.

Candida Lycett Green

*Author and journalist Candida Lycett Green chooses her six favourite books. Her book, **Over the Hills and Far Away**, about her journeys around Britain on horseback, is published by Doubleday.*

Issue 365: 6th July 2002

Great Expectations by Charles Dickens (Penguin). The most powerful and haunting opening of any book; the image of that misty Thames Estuary country is always with me. Wemmick is one of my favourite characters in fiction – I should very much like him to have been part of my life. Dickens is the master.

Madame Bovary by Gustave Flaubert (Penguin). This novel shocked and excited me when I first read it at 15. No man since Flaubert has captured a woman's predicament so perfectly. I particularly love the picture of Emma falling deeper in love with Rodolfo while they are riding spirited horses through the countryside.

The Four Quartets by T.S. Eliot (Faber & Faber). They are my fix. However awful things may be, to read a couple of pages makes everything all right again. I do not like to analyse why I love them so. I have my own private interpretation.

Henderson the Rain King by Saul Bellow (Penguin). Bellow is my favourite modern novelist by miles. Funnier, cleverer and gloomier than anyone else, he brings new light to the subjects of unhappiness and dissatisfaction and leaves me with a feeling of dark optimism. Here, he makes the failed and small-time Eugene Henderson realise he is capable of something great.

Slouching Towards Bethlehem by Joan Didion (Flamingo). Didion is my journalistic idol. In this collection of essays, she demonstrates her brilliance through devastatingly sharp and truthful glimpses of America in the Sixties.

A Very Private Eye edited by Hazel Holt and Hilary Pym (Out of print). This is the biography of Barbara Pym, a great and underrated novelist. Her courageous, funny, sad character and touching friendship with Philip Larkin is revealed through her own letters and diaries, edited by her sister and a friend. I have never read a life which felt so painfully real and true.

119

George MacDonald Fraser

The creator of the great Victorian rogue Flashman, George MacDonald Fraser, selects the six historical works that have most influenced him. His novel, **Flashman and the Angel of the Lord***, is published by HarperCollins.*

Issue 48: 27th April 1996

Captain Blood by Rafael Sabatini (Macmillan). Caught up in Monmouth's rebellion, mild Peter Blood becomes the terror of the Spanish Man. "A splendid novel in its own right which led me, at the age of 10, to the works of this great historical writer who showed me that history is an inexhaustible mine waiting to be exploited.

The Legend of Ulenspiegel by Charles de Coster (Heinemann). Translated into beautiful English by F.H. Atkinson, this is a Flemish epic which mingles the independence campaign of William the Silent with the exploits of the mythical folk-hero Tyl Ulenspiegel. One of those magical books which takes hold for a lifetime.

I, Claudius by Robert Graves (Penguin). A poet's fictionalized autobiography of the most intriguing of Roman emperors. A masterpiece of technique, accurately researched and honestly told, presented as modern fiction.

Henry 1V parts 1 and 2, and Henry V by William Shakespeare (Penguin). This trilogy of history plays are for me the summit of Shakespeare's achievement, with Falstaff as a bonus.

History of England by Lord Macaulay (Penguin). Simply the best work of history I've ever read. Reading it is like painting the Forth Bridge; whenever I finish it I start it again.

Tom Brown's Schooldays by Thomas Hughes (Puffin). Rough Education at the hands of the school bully Flashman at Victorian Rugby. How could I leave this out since Flashman has been the backbone of my livelihood for nearly 30 years ?

Sue MacGregor

*Sue MacGregor, former presenter on Radio 4's Today, chooses her favourite books about South Africa. MacGregor, who grew up in South Africa, has now published her autobiography, **Woman of Today**.*

Issue 380: 19th October 2002

Long Walk to Freedom by Nelson Mandela (Abacus). Of all the books about South Africa's apartheid years, and the regime change of 1994, this is the best. The section on Mandela's 18 years as a prisoner on Robben Island is central to understanding his character: you can smell the sea, feel the blinding sun, and share in his hope of release and reconciliation.

The Grass is Singing by Doris Lessing (Flamingo). Set in a neighbouring country – what was Southern Rhodesia – just after the war, this is the story of a marriage which ends in murder on a remote farm. One's heart bleeds for modern Zimbabwe, but you can see its seeds in this account of arid settler life.

A Fish Caught in Time by Samantha Weinberg (Fourth Estate). The fish is the coelacanth, which should have died out with the dinosaurs. In 1938 a South African museum curator called Marjorie Courtney-Latimer found a "queer-looking specimen" in a pile of fish on a trawler. This account of its subsequent identification as a living fossil, and of the search for more, is both gripping and scientifically fascinating.

Selected Stories by Nadine Gordimer (Bloomsbury). The Nobel Prize-winning author has refined and honed her style in her novels over the years, but perhaps her short stories are her most brilliantly consistent achievement.

Cry the Beloved Country by Alan Paton (Vintage). A classic novel of the "old" land, much of it based on Paton's own experience running a reformatory for delinquent boys. It is a heartbreaking tale of what happens when rural innocence meets the brutal reality of the city.

My Traitor's Heart by Rian Malan (Vintage). No one has described the soul of the Afrikaner better than this writer, a direct descendant of one of the master builders of apartheid, PM Daniel Francois Malan. Published in 1990, it is a vivid portrait of a people apparently heading towards Armageddon.

Andy McNab

*Andy McNab, former member of the SAS and author of **Bravo Two Zero** – a true account of his experiences in the Gulf War – chooses his six favourite books. His thriller, **Firewall**, is published by Bantam.*

Issue 275: 30th September 2000

The Deptford Trilogy by Robertson Davies (Penguin). I'm still trying to get my head around this book and I've read it twice. The three novels follow one man, from his childhood to his life as a soldier, teacher and magician. Like all good literature, there are just so many layers to it. I get more from the book each time I read it.

Touching the Void by Joe Simpson (Vintage). This is the true story of two mountaineers in the Andes. One of them has to make a snap decision: cut the rope and let his friend fall to almost-certain death, or don't cut it and get dragged over too. An incredible survival story.

Stick it up Your Punter – The Story of The Sun Newspaper by Peter Chippindale and Chris Horrie (Simon Schuster). One of my all-time favourite books. this is the complete lowdown on tabloid sleaze. From Elton John's record damages to the sinking of the Belgrano during the Falklands War.

King of the World by David Remnick (Vintage). Muhammad Ali has always been a hero of mine. Before reading this book, it was for his amazing boxing skill. After reading it, it was for the fact he spent his whole life fighting prejudice. Just as heroic.

Rex Deus by Tim Wallace-Murphy, Marilyn Hopkins and Graham Simmans (Element Books). Being a medieval history freak, I loved this book. It sets out to prove that Jesus's bloodline still exists and shows the role that the Knights Templar played in protecting that lineage.

Hitman by Max Kinnins (Hodder Headline). If you liked Trainspotting, you'll love this. It's about two drugged-up, would-be hitmen in north London bungling a planned murder. It's steeped in black humour and very, very funny.

John Major

*John Major, the former prime minister, chooses his six favourite books. His own book, **John Major: The Autobiography**, is published by Harper Collins.*

Issue 235: 18th December 1999

Below the Salt by Thomas Costain (Out of print). A charming tale set at the time of the Magna Carta that I first read when I was 11. It is told by an eminent American senator who miraculously recalls an earlier life in medieval England and a love that he lost.

How Green was My Valley by Richard Llewellyn (Penguin). One of the greatest books ever written. The hardships and pleasures of life in a Welsh mining village as seen through the eyes of an impressionable boy. Immensely moving.

The White Company by Sir Arthur Conan Doyle (Wordsworth). Conan Doyle didn't only write about Sherlock Holmes. My father loved this tale of a company of Saxon bowmen fighting in the Hundred Years' War during the 14th century, and so do I.

Past Caring by Robert Goddard (Transworld). This was Robert Goddard's first book and I was entranced by it. Intrigue, mystery and treachery mingle with the finer virtues in this riveting tale of why an eminent politician disappeared from public life.

The Unlikely Spy by Daniel Silva (Orion). Set in 1944, this gripping thriller follows the attempts by a college professor to stop a female German spy uncovering the secrets of D-Day. A really authentic portrait of espionage with a thrilling, believable climax. One of the best novels of recent years.

A Horseman Riding By by R.F. Delderfield (Sceptre). Delderfield's masterpiece about an ex-soldier's life after World War I as he restores a derelict estate in a Devon valley. Wonderful characterisation.

Valerie Martin

*Writer Valerie Martin chooses her five favourite books. Her novel, **Property**, which won the 2003 Orange Prize, is published by Abacus.*

Issue 428: 27th September 2003

Madame Bovary by Gustave Flaubert (Penguin) The master casts a pitiless eye upon the interior life of a provincial charmer. As Flaubert wrote to his mistress, Louise Colet, "there is no such thing as subject – style in itself being an absolute manner of seeing things". This cautionary tale about the perils of a romantic education is proof of that assertion.

Naomi by Junichiro Tanizaki (Vintage) This short, tantalising novel is sometimes called "the Japanese Lolita". Tanizaki's later masterpiece The Makioka Sisters may be a more complex and imaginative feat, but for sheer narrative drive this tale of Galatea's revenge is relentlessly thrilling.

New Grub Street by George Gissing (Penguin) A harrowing chronicle of writer's block, Gissing's most popular novel also contains a rare portrait of male friendship at its best. When Harold Biffen, author of the undervalued epic Mr Bailey, Grocer, rushes to the bedside of his dying friend, Edwin Reardon, who has literally been killed by the exigencies of the three-volume novel, I weep every time.

Mrs Palfrey at the Claremont by Elizabeth Taylor (Virago) I'd be hard put to choose six favourites just from among Taylor's novels, but Mrs Palfrey, which explores the indignities visited upon the elderly at a hotel that is not quite their last stop on earth, is high on that list. As in all of this too-neglected author's work, an amusing, yet chilling world is here delineated with elegance and wit.

Disgrace by J.M. Coetzee (Vintage) Expelled from his university, David Lurie, the unrepentant harassing professor, finds something that is not exactly solace when he moves in with his daughter, a smallholder of independent views and not much interest in her father's life crises. Coetzee is always scathing, but this unsettling novel is his most thorough scouring to date of what passes, in a world of hypocrites, for moral certitude.

China Miéville

*The science fiction writer China Miéville chooses six of his favourite books from what he considers to be the weird fiction category. His novel, **The Scar**, is published by Macmillan.*

Issue 407: 3rd May 2003

Death to the Pigs: Selected Writings by Benjamin Péret (Bison Books). Péret was a baby-faced timebomb, a revolutionary socialist, poet and theorist, who stayed absolutely faithful to the insurrectionary aesthetic of Surrealism. Hilarious, shocking, sad and touching in changing proportions, it is always an inspirational mongrel of politics and poetry.

Strange Evil by Jane Gaskell (Out of print). Written when Gaskell was 14, this book has the excesses you'd expect from an adolescent author. But in its fraught and disturbing version of fairyland and its truly original monstrosities and chimeras, this is a book of vastly greater power than many adult works.

The Island of Dr Moreau by H.G. Wells (House of Stratus). Wells's towering achievement. In terse prose, he mercilessly distorts the didacticism, convention and expectation of "progressive" Victorian morals. No wonder Jorge Luis Borges called this book "an atrocious miracle".

Stranger Things Happen by Kelly Link (Small Beer Press). The most exciting of the new wave of American writers of science fiction and fantasy fiction. This collection of short stories is the most literate and exciting new work I've read for a long time, in any genre. Well worth hunting down online, available at www.kellylink.net.

Jane Eyre by Charlotte Brontë (Penguin). A vividly uncanny book, notwithstanding its apparent lack of supernatural content, full of passages that provoke real existential fear. For those not hamstrung by genre snobbery, this is surely the greatest horror novel ever written.

Black Sunlight by Dambudzo Marechera (Heinemann). The most intense and unremitting work by the troubled genius of Zimbabwean literature. A brief, darkly surreal and apocalyptic novel that blows apart hidebound conceptions of the African novel.

Deborah Moggach

*Deborah Moggach has written 13 novels and numerous television screenplays. She has adapted her novel **Tulip Fever** into a screenplay for Steven Spielberg. Here she chooses her six favourite books.*

Issue 210: 26th June 1999

Like Life by Lorrie Moore (Faber). Lorrie Moore is my favourite writer – any of her collections of short stories are equally blissful. She writes with a sort of exhilarating despair about relationships – their hopelessness, and how, despite all the odds, we keep trying. She is terribly funny, and cuts to the quick.

The Accidental Tourist by Anne Tyler (Vintage). A man whose son has been shot by a random killer sees his marriage collapse and finds solace with an eccentric dog-trainer. I think this is Anne Tyler's finest novel – a richly human exploration of the nature of grief, and how one tries to make sense of the senseless. It also has literature's best portrait of a dog.

The Siege of Krishnapur by J.G. Farrell (Phoenix). This marvellous novel won the Booker Prize in the Seventies. It's about an embattled British colony defending itself against an Indian uprising, and is an engrossing, hilarious and subtle examination of human frailty and courage.

Middlemarch by George Eliot (Penguin). I love this novel for its largeness of vision and its intelligence. Reading it is like stepping into a parallel life to one's own – a more engrossing one – with a large cast of absorbing characters.

Rabbit Run by John Updike (Penguin). I've picked this novel at random – in fact, any of Updike's would do. Before I start a novel I like to read a few pages of superlative prose – Updike or Nabokov – just to sharpen the taste buds.

Injury Time by Beryl Bainbridge (Penguin). The same goes for Beryl Bainbridge. I started reading her novels when I began writing my own, and she taught me a great deal about having a singular voice, and keeping an eye on the oddities of life.

George Monbiot

*George Monbiot, the environmentalist, author and Guardian columnist, chooses his six favourite books. His book, **The Age of Consent: A Manifesto For A New World Order**, is published by Flamingo.*

Issue 414: 21st June 2003

Selected Poems by John Clare (Out of print). The beautiful and tragic work of Britain's most shamefully neglected poet. The poems first document his ecstatic engagement with the land, and then, as the landscape is divided up and ripped apart by enclosure, the creeping madness which accompanies his despair at its destruction.

Anna Karenina by Leo Tolstoy (Penguin). Levin's scything of the hayfield is the most compelling descrip-tion I've come across in any work of prose. Like all Tolstoy novels, Anna Karenina breaks down a bit towards the end, but still manages to show us the lives of its people as if we are seeing them for ourselves.

Dead Souls by Nikolai Gogol (Penguin). A mad, rambling, but staggeringly brilliant novel, by a mad and rambling man. Like Dostoevsky, Gogol manages in some places precisely to capture a character in just a sentence or two – look out for the description of the officials banqueting on fish.

The Rights of Man by Thomas Paine (Wordsworth Editions). The definitive defence of democracy and, arguably, the finest piece of political writing ever published in English. Paine skewers his opponents with agile and often hilarious arguments, while laying out a fiercely convincing democratic philosophy.

An Insular Possession by Timothy Mo (Paddleless Press). It forces you to keep asking yourself whether you are reading fiction or a well-researched history. It is, of course, both, and creates a world so real that it is hard not to believe that every incident happened.

The Future of Money by Bernard Lietaer (Century). Lietaer was once the world's top currency trader, but stepped back to ponder what he and his colleagues were doing to the world, and how the global money supply could be designed to protect people's livelihoods and the environment, rather than destroying them. A brilliant, visionary book.

127

Sheridan Morley

*Sheridan Morley, drama critic and broadcaster, chooses his eight favourite books. His memoirs, **Asking For Trouble**, is published by Hodder & Stoughton.*

Issue 385: 23rd November 2002

The Simon Crisp Diaries by Christopher Matthew (Coronet). Though Matthew is now more famous for Now We Are Sixty, Crisp is his masterpiece – a latter-day Pooter surviving the Seventies, or rather not.

Bollywood Boy by Justine Hardy (John Murray). Yes she's a first cousin, but this is still the best fictionalised drama-doc about the Indian film industry in all its Gothic eccentricity.

The Gladys Society by Sandi Toksvig (Little, Brown). Touching and funny account of our favourite Great Dane going back to the America of her childhood and searching for its survivors.

Sacred Monsters, Sacred Masters by John Richardson (Pimlico). A brilliant collection of essays on Capote, Dali, Picasso, Warhol etc.

The Unexpurgated Beaton by Cecil Beaton (Weidenfeld & Nicolson). All the rude and dirty bits that Hugo Vickers had to delete from Beaton's diaries in his lifetime, available now because the targets are all beyond reach of their libel lawyers.

Things My Mother Never Told Me by Blake Morrison (Chatto & Windus). After And When Did You Last See Your Father?, Morrison continues what is quite simply the best current series of family portraits – all written in love and regret, recollection and resentment.

Brewer's Rogues, Villains and Eccentrics by Willie Donaldson (Cassell). Donaldson has come up with the funniest book of the year, unless you count (albeit unintentionally) John Birt's memoirs. This is a rich and rare catalogue of bigamists, tricksters, gangsters, acid-bath murderers, highwaymen and others who have added to the gaiety of nations.

My Life as Me by Barry Humphries (Michael Joseph). The fascinating second volume of his memoirs, in which, finally, Barry himself comes out from under the skirts of Dame Edna.

Jan Morris

*Jan Morris is an historian and travel writer. Her books **Fisher Face**, "a capricious love letter to an admiral", and **Over Europe**, "a subjective evocation of 50 years in Europe", are published by Viking Penguin.*

Issue 90: 22nd February 1997

The Nigger of the Narcissus by Joseph Conrad (Penguin). This short book, so its author said, "aspires…. Humbly to the condition of art". It must be the best sea story ever written, by a master of not just English prose, but of human understanding.

The Possessed by Fyodor Doestoevsky (Vintage). My grandfather's copy, in Constance Garnett's translation, has been in my library for as long as I can remembers, but it was only this year that I immersed myself in its extraordinary take of Russian intrigue, self-deception, comedy, tragedy and love – at once mysterious, prophetic, satirical and genuinely tear-jerking.

Buddenbrooks by Thomas Mann (Mandarin). I never read this until I became interested in the city of Lübeck. Then I realized, not for the first time, that a novel is by far the best medium for civic evocation, and I admired it for its flavour of Lübeck life and majestic plot and characterisation.

Ulysses by James Joyce (Penguin). I must have tried a dozen times to read this terrific but largely incomprehensible work, only to read it in my 70th year. I would have failed until in Dublin I found Harry Blamires' admirable crib The Bloomsday Book. Since then I've never looked back.

The Radetzky March by Joseph Roth (Penguin). This Australian masterpiece about life in the fading Habsburg Empire has hung about the edges of my consciousness for decades, but I would not have missed it for the world.

Babbit by Sinclair Lewis (Random House). I first went to the American Middle West in 1953, but I never got around to this marvelously readable assessment of its values until the Nineties. It is rather a period piece now, but the satire still hits home.

Blake Morrison

*Author and poet Blake Morrison chooses his six favourite books of the century. His own books include his memoir, **And When Did You Last See Your Father?** and **Selected Poems** both published by Granta.*

Issue 229: 6th November 1999

My Father and Myself by J.R. Ackerley (Pimlico). Literary editor of the Listener, Ackerley left behind one little masterpiece, an account of his duplicitous father (who secretly kept two families), and of his own encounters with gay lovers and dogs. The candour still shocks 30 years on.

The Tin Drum by Günter Grass (Vintage). At last awarded the Nobel Prize for Literature, Grass first made his mark in 1959 with this novel, memorable not only for its story of a boy who refuses to grow, but for its sensual images: a child's-eye view of a Nazi rostrum; a horse's head wriggling with eels; sherbet fizz licked from the stomach of a beautiful girl.

Ulysses by James Joyce (Penguin). The best book I know for opening at random to find sentences of forgotten brilliance or unexpected wit. This day in the life of Dublin remains the most innovative novel of our century, not least for its odyssey in human consciousness and for Molly Bloom's final affirming "yes".

Collected Poems by T.S. Eliot (Faber). It was reading Eliot as a teenager that first got me interested in poetry, and for all the recent demonising of him as a cruel husband and an anti-Semite, I continue to be haunted by the cold beauty of The Wasteland and the wise music of the Four Quartets.

Selected Letters of Philip Larkin (Faber). Although a sad and grumpy librarian eaten up by "the maggot of loneliness, the maggot of romantic illusion, the maggot of sexual desire", Larkin was also one of the funniest writers ever born, as these frank and often foul-mouthed letters (the best of them to Kingsley Amis) show.

The Counterlife by Philip Roth (Knopf). Roth has re-emerged as one of the great US novelists of our time, outshining even Bellow and Updike. This novel is perhaps his most radical, a book that plays games and switches narrators but is never merely tricksy.

John Mortimer

*Novelist and playwright John Mortimer chooses his six favourite books. His book, **Rumpole Rests His Case**, saw the return of the famous barrister after a six-year absence and is published by Penguin.*

Issue 329: 20th October 2001

Don Juan by Lord Byron (Penguin). An unfinished novel written in complex stanzas, romantic, ironic, comic and satirical. The whole work celebrates his love of women and his hatred of hypocrisy and the Lake poets. He thought of Coleridge explaining metaphysics to the world and wrote: "I wish he would explain his explanation."

The Decline and Fall of the Roman Empire by Edward Gibbon (Penguin, in 3 volumes). Impossible to cope with it all, perhaps, but Gibbon's account of Christianity taking over the Roman Empire is a masterpiece of ironic comedy. He tells us that all the religions practised in the Empire were considered equally true by the people, equally false by the philosopher and equally useful by the magistrate. This produced an admirable degree of religious concord.

Scoop by Evelyn Waugh (Penguin). This is a wholly successful novel, continually funny but with moments of sadness when the author of The Countryside Column becomes a war correspondent by mistake.

Eminent Victorians by Lytton Strachey (Penguin). Strachey is the one true genius of Bloomsbury. His prose is here to be loved and learned from. He is at his best elegantly pricking the bubble reputations of Victorian monuments.

The Lady in the Lake by Raymond Chandler (Penguin). Chandler wrote his paragraphs on separate slips of paper to make sure he had something comic or surprising in each one. Most of the time he succeeds brilliantly. Revel in the writing and don't spend too much time trying to work out the plot.

A Moveable Feast by Ernest Hemingway (Vintage). A beautifully written memory of when Hemingway was an unknown writer in Paris. The seeds of what we do are in us, says Hemingway, but the soil and manure is better for those who make jokes.

131

James Naughtie

*James Naughtie, who presents Today and Bookclub on BBC Radio 4, chooses his six favourite books about America. His book, **The Accidental American: Tony Blair and the Presidency**, is published by Macmillan.*

Issue 479: 25th September 2004

First, one of the great political biographies of our time, the third volume of Robert A. Caro's riveting life of **Lyndon Johnson. Master of the Senate** (Vintage) takes the story from his election to the Senate, up to the 1960 election, and paints the most detailed and fascinating picture of the civil rights struggle and the politics of Capitol Hill. Brilliant, irresistible and vast.

If LBJ was the most enigmatic of modern presidents, part-monster and part-progressive hero, one of the great fictional figures in American literature is Willie Stark, the corrupt governor in Robert Penn Warren's novel **All the King's Men** (Prion) which is to the south what The Last Hurrah is to Boston.

Stepping back into the real world, the second biography to recommend is Edmund Morris's **Theodore Rex** (HarperCollins), which brings Teddy Roosevelt and the first decade of the 20th century to life, a time of invention and bull-headed determination, told with a wry understanding of the wiles of politics.

And the voice of the Sixties that still stirs memories of the boldness and wildness of the time is the book of essays that spawned a new kind of writing, which is as fresh now as it was when we all picked it up for the first time and fell under its spell – Tom Wolfe's **The Kandy-Colored, Tangerine-Flake Streamline Baby** (Picador).

But one book still causes me (reluctantly) to put aside The Great Gatsby or Light in August, and that is, of course, **Moby Dick** (Penguin). Dense, rambling, hypnotic and exhilarating, it's still the best depiction in adventure of that strange and rampant thing, the American spirit.

In journalism rather than history, I still turn to Norman Mailer, whom I think of as journalist rather than novelist, and **Armies of the Night** (Out of print) is the best account from the Sixties of the Vietnam agony among the young.

Derek Nimmo

The actor and producer Derek Nimmo chooses his six favourite books.

Issue 157: 13th June 1998

Armadillo by William Boyd (Hamish Hamilton). Boyd's deadly comic book is deeply compelling. Nothing is as it first appears. An acute exploration of the bizarre nature of contemporary life by one of our greatest contemporary writers.

A Kentish Lad by Frank Muir (Bantam Press). For more than 25 years, Frank Muir, in partnership with Dennis Norden, produced some of the most sparkling, original comedy ever written for radio and television. This hugely endearing autobiography, complete with anecdotes, by a master raconteur is a truly life-enhancing experience.

Partridge Catalogue – Acquisitions 1998 (Published by Partridge, 144/146 New Bond Street). Yearly Catalogue compiled by Lucy Morton for this Fine-Art gallery. As always, the most extraordinary piece of scholarship.

A Gilt-Edged Life by Edmund de Rothschild (John Murray). A memoir by the eldest surviving male descendant of N.M. Rothschild, who founded the English branch of the bank in 1798. A key witness to all the changing fortunes of his family.

Dear Bill by W.F. Deedes (Macmillan). Lord Deedes' memoirs provide a unique and idiosyncratic perception of matters political and social, British and global, for the greater part of this century.

A History of Architecture by Sir Banister Fletcher (Butterworth Architecture). I recently replaced a dog-eared edition won as a school prize 50 years ago. I now have a brand new edition – essential reading for any lover of architecture.

John Julius Norwich

*John Julius Norwich, the historian and author, chooses his six favourite travel books. His book, **The Illustrated Christmas Cracker**, is published by Doubleday.*

Issue 391: 11th January 2003

Brazilian Adventure by Peter Fleming (Northwestern UP).
In 1925 the author answered an ad in The Times about an expedition to central Brazil to ascertain the fate of the lost explorer Col Fawcett. The result was a near-fiasco but the book is a comic triumph.

The Road to Oxiana by Robert Byron (Penguin). Byron Mark II, as brilliant and even more maddening than his noble predecessor, died at 36 when his ship was torpedoed in 1941. Together with The Byzantine Achievement (written in his early twenties) this hugely entertaining diary of a journey to Persia and Afghanistan in search of the origins of Islamic architecture had an enormous impact on me in my youth.

Journey's Echo by Freya Stark (Out of print). Stark was another of the great stylists of the last century. This slim volume is an anthology of her best travel writing. It proves that however great a traveller she was, as a writer she was greater still.

From the Holy Mountain by William Dalrymple (Flamingo). The most talented of our younger generation of travel writers explores all the oldest Christian communities of the Levant, beginning with Mt Athos, and proceeding through Turkey, Syria, Lebanon, Israel and Jordan to Egypt. The story he tells is a sad one – they are all doomed – but he is incapable of writing a dull page.

Eothen by A.W. Kinglake (Konneman UK). Kinglake travelled through Egypt and the Levant, and published this account of his adventures in 1844. It is still one of the funniest travel books ever printed.

A Time of Gifts by Patrick Leigh Fermor (John Murray). The first volume of an account of the author's walk to Constantinople, beginning in 1933 when he was 18. There is no more virtuoso writer of English alive today: try his description of the Munich beer-cellar – a hilarious tour de force.

John O'Farrell

*John O'Farrell, author of **Things Can Only Get Better** and writer behind shows such as **Have I Got News For You**, chooses his six favourite funny novels. His new book, **Global Village Idiot**, is published by Doubleday*

Issue 331: 3rd November 2001

Catch 22 by Joseph Heller (Vintage). War is mad, apparently. But Heller says it with great wit, a compelling narrative and fantastic characters. When told that he had not written anything as good since, Heller allegedly replied, "No, but neither has anyone else." Good for him.

Billy Liar by Keith Waterhouse (Penguin). Billy Fisher is an inspiration to us all. He's a feckless wastrel who tells unsustainable lies (claiming relations have just had a leg amputated is a particular favourite) and yet you empathise with him from start to finish. His father's use of the word "bloody" seven times in every sentence never stops being funny.

Lucky Jim by Kingsley Amis (Penguin). A wonderfully warm and enjoyable book set in second-division academia. Another low-achieving first-person narrator (or maybe this was the prototype) whose life is constantly knocked off course by the infuriating characters around him. The best thing Kingsley Amis ever produced after Martin.

Breathing Lessons by Anne Tyler (Vintage). Tyler's characters are simultaneously funny and sad, heroic and pathetic, and none more so than Maggie and Ira. A mundane car journey reveals all the infuriating insecurities and well-meaning ineptitude of her wonderful heroine and you end up thinking you've known this family all your life.

The Rotters Club by Jonathan Coe (Penguin). A very funny book about an all-boys school in the Seventies, set against the political backdrop of the time – all the horrors of the IRA, the National Front and knitted tank tops are in there. The sixth formers having sex with the sports bag could have been me (but my sports bag would have wanted to wait a bit).

Prisoner 49475 by Jeffrey Archer. This book doesn't exist yet, but something like it will in a few years' time and I'm sure it'll give us more laughs than all the others put together.

Maggie O'Farrell

The author Maggie O'Farrell chooses her six favourite books. Her own novel, **After You'd Gone**, *is published by Review.*

Issue 308: 26th May 2001

The Private Memoirs and Confessions of a Justified Sinner by James Hogg (Penguin). Apart from having the best title ever, this is a terrifying psychological novel about being haunted by a protean Other. I'm not sure why, but the Scottish have always had the edge when it comes to tales of split identities and doppelgangers.

American Pastoral by Philip Roth (Vintage). I'd find it hard to say which Roth is my favourite, but I'm fascinated by the inverted spiralling structure of this one, and the perfectly imperfect narration of the Swede Levov.

The Outsider by Albert Camus (Penguin). I was obsessed with this novel when I was a teenager. Aged 16, I'd never come across anything like it. Its weird tempo, its mesmerising narrator and its intensely physical take on the world stunned me – and still does.

The Yellow Wallpaper by Charlotte Perkins Gilman (Virago). This tiny novella, first published in 1892, is an incredible portrait of a doomed marriage. A young woman, confined to her room by her over-solicitous husband, is driven slowly mad by the heavily patterned wallpaper.

Hallucinating Foucault by Patricia Duncker (Picador). This is a strange and vivid story about a young student going in search of his thesis subject, a vanished French writer. The lightness of the narrative belies its larger questions about love and sex and sanity.

Jane Eyre by Charlotte Bronte (Penguin). This is not only the best Victorian novel but a book that has everything – an indomitable female narrator, a gripping love story, and a mad woman in the attic. I love it because it's furious and passionate and fierce. And because I fancy Mr Rochester.

Tom Paulin

Tom Paulin teaches English at Hertford College, Oxford.
*His collection of poems, **The Wind Dog**, is published by Faber.*
Here he chooses his six favourite books.

Issue 212: 10th July 1999

Photo: Barney Cokeliss

Paradise Lost by John Milton (Penguin). Milton's great republican epic is a coded attack on the Stuarts and a vision of English history during the Civil War, Common-wealth and early Restoration. It is the most sublime poem in the English language – I teach it every year and always learn something new from the experience.

Ulysses by James Joyce (Penguin). I first read Joyce's magnificent comic epic as a student in Belfast – subsequent readings have taught me that it, too, is a supreme republican work of art. It imagines an Ireland which effortlessly transcends sectarian and racist politics.

Clarissa by Samuel Richardson (Haughton Mifflin). I think this and Ulysses are the two greatest novels in English. It represents English history from a puritan point of view and is at the same time a highly complex psychological novel which vindicates Clarissa's "native dignity" against the cynical, autocratic values represented by her would-be seducer Lovelace.

Poems and Prose of Gerard Manley Hopkins (Penguin). The Penguin edition of Hopkins with the Ivon Hitchens cover is one of my sacred books. The lift, the kick, the vision, the wildness and discipline of Hopkins are like no one else.

Collected Poems of W.B. Yeats (Macmillan). The experience of reading Yeats is caught for me in these lines from that despairing love poem The Cold Heaven: "I cried and trembled and rocked to and fro / Riddled with light." I love the clatter of consonants in Yeats and the uplifting beauty of the vowels.

The Collected Poems of Robert Frost (Penguin). Frost is a vernacular genius, the master of sentence-sound, dark, mischievous, pastoral and political. His poems became a vocation from the moment I first heard a record of him reading After Apple-Picking which my English teacher played us at school.

Ben Pimlott

Ben Pimlott, historian and warden of Goldsmiths College, University of London, chooses his five favourite books. His own work includes two biographies: **Harold Wilson** *and* **The Queen**, *both published by HarperCollins.*

Issue 245: 4th March 2000

The Great War and Modern Memory by Paul Fussell (Oxford University Press). This brilliant study makes literary criticism seem worthwhile. Fussell uses turn-of-the-century popular, as well as literary, writing to show how words and images not only anticipate events, but help to create them. At the same time, he pinpoints the euphemisms of 20th century conflict ("the fallen", and so forth) that chillingly distort the way we think about slaughter.

The Sword of Honour Trilogy by Evelyn Waugh (Penguin). Waugh's cluster of wartime novels are the best books he wrote, and the best literature on World War II. The picaresque adventures of the conservative but amenable Guy Crouchback give poignant support to the cock-up theory of all military endeavour.

The Sound and the Fury by William Faulkner (Vintage). Faulkner's stunning evocation of the emotions of an idiot is the most painfully acute novel written this century. No other work makes such a convincing case for the mentally impaired, or shows so movingly that inarticulate feelings can be as powerful as those expressed in words.

Queen Victoria by Lytton Strachey (Penguin). This novel-like study of the queen whose name became synonymous with 19th century prudery is the best-written English biography of the 20th century. Strachey's camp yet affectionate portrayal of a tartan-hugging, domesticity-loving bourgeois makes it infuriatingly difficult to think of her as anything else.

The Witch Craze of the Sixteenth and Seventeenth Centuries by Hugh Trevor Roper (Penguin). Trevor Roper is a historian who writes with wicked, provocative clarity. He argues that a belief in witchcraft was not an incidental aspect of our forebears' mental furniture, but an essential part of it. And he warns that thoughts we take for granted may end up looking criminally absurd a few generations hence.

Henry Porter

*Henry Porter, the journalist and author, chooses his five favourite film comedies. His first thriller, **Remembrance Day**, is published by Orion.*

Issue 188: 23rd January 1999

Monsieur Hulot's Holiday. It seems extraordinary that Jacques Tati's masterpiece about a French holiday resort, filmed on a budget which would barely cover Demi Moore's on-location mineral water bill, has not been bettered in the 50-odd years since it was made. Monsieur Hulot is a remedy for depression only equalled by swimming with dolphins.

I'm All Right Jack. With the exception of the Carry On films, I'm happy with almost any British comedy made in the first 20 years after the war. I chose this one because of Peter Sellers' performance as the union leader but also because of the presence of Denis Price.

Mon Oncle. It seems unfair to give two places to Jacques Tati. (But, with a little more room, I'd even include Tati's other films Jour de Fête and Playtime.) Mon Oncle features Tati as Hulot (above), this time wrestling with the materialism of the modern world. A beautifully designed film with Tati skidding between apology and panic and hopeless generosity of spirit.

The Odd Couple. I have a weakness for Walter Matthau and therefore include this film, although Jack Lemmon's character drives me crazy to the point I wish Matthau would murder him. But Matthau's hangdog, raging, lecherous expressions make me laugh and in this film you see the full range.

Withnail and I. At the heart of great comedy often lies the doomed ambition of one character. In the case of Bruce Robinson's classic it belongs to Withnail, the individualist actor – played by Richard E. Grant – who is too true to himself to make any start on a career. Withnail's attempt to drive down a motorway having had no experience at the wheel is without parallel in the annals of automotive humour.

Anthony Price

*Cold War novelist Anthony Price chooses his six favourite books. His book, **The Eyes of the Fleet**, is a history set in the Napoleonic era and is published by Hutchinson.*

Issue 313: 30th June 2001

A Social History of the Navy 1793-1815 by Michael Lewis (out of print). Where does one go after Patrick O'Brien or the much superior C.S. Forester? But here, anyway, are the real Horn-blowers and Aubreys – and (more to the point) Nelson and his real navy. Never have facts and figures been more elegantly, ingeniously and often amusingly adduced to show how Britannia ruled the waves in the era of Trafalgar.

Puck of Pook's Hill by Rudyard Kipling (House of Stratus). Puck is no "sugar-and-shake-your-head" fairy impostor: he never talks down to children (or adults) and his magic still works a treat. Lord Geoffrey's Fancy by Alfred Duggan (out of print). Actually, any Duggan historical novel will do (Knight With Armour is the best account of the First Crusade outside Runciman), but this picture of 13th century Greece under Frankish feudalism after the Fourth Crusade shows his technique to perfection.

Alamein to Zem Zem by Keith Douglas (Faber). Arguably the best of the young poets to see action in World War II, Douglas survived just long enough to leave this unique portrait of an old-fashioned yeomanry regiment in North Africa. His poetic imagery is equalled only by his youthful candour.

Subaltern's War by Charles Edmonds, aka Charles Carrington (Out of print). Forget Graves and Sassoon, however good. This worm's-eye view of the Somme in 1916 and Ypres in 1917 by a soldier too young to follow his regiment to France in 1915 is unsurpassed for his honesty and the vividness of his recollections.

The Histories by Tacitus (Penguin). No single year in history quite surpasses AD 69 – "the Year of the Four Emperors" – which followed the death of Nero and ended with the triumph of Vespasian. And no one can say that Tacitus doesn't give it the full dramatic treatment it deserves.

140

Libby Purves

*Libby Purves, the broadcaster, journalist and author, selects six books splendidly out of tune with the age. Her novel, **Regatta**, is published by Flame.*

Photo: Nick Davies

Issue 256: 20th May 2000

King Solomon's Mines by Rider Haggard (Puffin). At seven I fantasised about standing alongside noble Zulus with Allan Quatermain, slaying foes with an axe and discovering lost diamond mines ruled over by eerie tribes. Now I know that this would have been disgracefully imperialistic behaviour, but it was fun at the time.

Mansfield Park by Jane Austen (Penguin). The one which feminist Austenians hate, because Fanny Price suffers in silence and deploys Christian fortitude rather than rebellion. Its power to annoy is proved by the hideous hash made of it by the new film, with a ridiculously feisty flashing-eyed Fanny.

Trustee from the Toolroom by Nevil Shute (Vintage). Shute celebrated the anorak. In this book the hero is painfully undistinguished, except in model engineering, but becomes a hero of epic proportions. An adult fairy-tale.

Scott-King's Modern Europe by Evelyn Waugh (Out of print). A classics master invited on a bogus academic conference is caught up in the corrupt chaos of postwar Europe. Back at school he refuses to switch to a more relevant subject: "I think, Headmaster, it would be very wicked indeed to do anything to fit a boy for the modern world."

The Woodlanders by Thomas Hardy (Penguin). The same sad fate befell this one; the film industry couldn't believe that Grace would go back to her bastard of a husband and leave only Marty South to mourn Giles. So they wrecked the end instead, out of sheer temper.

The Little Princess by Frances Hodgson Burnett (Hodder). And with this book the film industry brought the father back to life, thus robbing the story of its Victorian dignity and modern children of a powerful myth.

Mary Quant

*Mary Quant, the fashion designer, chooses five hugely enjoyable recent indulgences. Her book, **Classic Make-up & Beauty**, is published by Dorling Kindersley.*

Issue 397: 22nd February 2003

Editor: A Memoir by Max Hastings (Pan). Max Hastings's autobiography of his years as editor of The Daily Telegraph is riveting stuff. I so admired his tough, honest directness and found myself longing to be 6'4" and male. Although it did occur to me that the Queen has amazing charisma at 5'4".

Bad Blood by Lorna Sage (Fourth Estate). I find it a great mistake to pick up this autobiography because I then can't put it down. Mad, extraordinary and quite beautiful, her childhood is surreally compulsive. Post-war provincial Britain for teenage Lorna was gloomy, inhibitive and prudish. How right she was – we all were – to kick it.

Colette: Secrets of the Flesh by Judith Thurman (Bloomsbury). I enjoyed this book for many reasons, but most of all because I am fascinated to know what it was like to live in Paris under the Nazi occupation. Colette lived in the centre of Paris and her husband was Jewish. The daily risks of living were lethal. Her name and stunning self-confidence helped, but the terror and cold were awesome.

Love from Nancy: the Letters of Nancy Mitford edited by Charlotte Mosley (Hodder & Stoughton). I have Nancy Mitford's letters to hand to dip into like a bag of crisps. She never fails to perk one up and egg one on to a glass of wine. Her generous wit and bounce still affects and her hard edge still shocks. I love the way she knows to indulge herself with a Dior couture dress from time to time. Too sensible for an Englishwoman.

Experience by Martin Amis (Vintage). This autobiography – largely about his father, Kingsley – is just the best treat. It's like eating the richest, most delicious Christmas cake. You just have to chew it very slowly not to miss a currant and long to chew it over and over again. I knew Kingsley a bit and yes, he's got it – including the scary bits. The dentist part should be compulsory reading for every dentist. I laughed till my teeth ached.

Frederic Raphael

Screenwriter and author Frederic Raphael chooses five favourite books.
*His book, **The Benefits of Doubt: Essays**, is published by Carcanet, while his*
*translation of **Petronius's Satyrica** is published by the Folio Society.*

Issue 433: 1st November 2003

The Poems of Constantine Cavafy (Princeton University Press). In Sherrard and Keeley's translation, there is the luxury of English facing the Greek, so I can pretend to read without help. Work in a foreign language is the great mental anaesthetic: in Cavafy's Hellas, you find a world without too manifest connections with today, yet pitilessly relevant.

The Great Gatsby by F. Scott Fitzgerald (Penguin). Here nothing is unknown, but the bitter-sweet myth never loses its charm, nor the sense of pity for Scott Fitzgerald, who wrote his masterpiece so young that everything that followed in his (short) life was an anti-climax.

Byron's Letters and Journals edited by Leslie A. Marchand (Harvard University Press). There may be differing views about Byron's poetry, and all have something to be said for them except, maybe, Wilson Knight's wish to match him with Shakespeare. The letters are shameless and beyond criticism: you are invited to love and hate "poor dear me" and you may well do both.

The History of the Decline and Fall of the Roman Empire by Edward Gibbon (Penguin). A great literary caucus race: you may join in and leave off where you choose. He was not a great stylist in the Augustan tradition but a master of the footnote, which he practised with mordant, sparing genius.

A la Recherche du Temps Perdu by Marcel Proust (Fixot). I have to choose Proust for the same reasons: a favourite is something you go back to and find fresh, or forgotten. There is a timeless relevance in Proust, whose snobbery is not of a kind to fawn on Becks or Posh but reminds us of the vanity of being a fan, whether of nobs or slobs. A man may tire of Marcel's imperfect sub-junctives, but what an eye, and what an ear!

Piers Paul Read

Journalist and author Piers Paul Read chooses his favourite books. His novel, **Knights of the Cross**, *is published by Weidenfeld & Nicolson .*

Issue 125: October 1997

Vanity Fair by William Thackeray (Penguin). A sparkling antidote to the heavy and sentimental novels of Dickens and Hardy. Witty and psychologically perceptive, above all in its depiction of women. Becky Sharpe equals Flaubert's Emma Bovary or Tolstoy's Anna Karenina.

My Past and Thoughts by Alexander Herzen (Out of print). Herzen left Russia in 1848 when he inherited his father's fortune and led the expatriate opposition to the Tsar from Paris and later London. His superb memoirs give a fascinating insight into revolutionary circles of the period, and contain poignant

Epitaph of a Small Winner (Bloomsbury). A concise, elegant and humorous novel by the 19th-century Brazilian author Machado de Assis, who has been described as the most disenchanted writer in western literature.

The Decline and Fall of the Roman Empire by Edward Gibbon (Penguin). Described by Gibbon's former fiancée, Mme Necker, as a bridge that carries us from the ancient to the modern world.

The Charterhouse of Parma by Stendhal (Penguin). An obeisance to my youth, when I liked to imagine myself as one of Stendhal's rebellious heroes. No other writer equals Stendhal's pace and zest.

Pensées by Blaise Pascal (Penguin). No trace of wishful thinking in this highly intellectual apologia for the Catholic religion. Sceptical, ironic, aphoristic – a powerful refutation of the modern notion that faith is for simpletons.

Griff Rhys Jones

The comedian Griff Rhys Jones chooses six of the best books he has read recently.

Issue 173: 3rd October 1998

History of My Life by Giacomo Casanova (Johns Hopkins University Press). Perhaps all the best diaries were written before 1800. Casanova's recently appeared in 12 paperback volumes, and there has been nothing as boastful, silly, sexy or stylish until Glen Hoddle came to print. The length gives you endless opportunities to speculate on whether the Chevalier de Seingalt is actually making it all up.

The Rings of Saturn by Willam Sebald (Harvill). A professor of German walks down part of the Suffolk coast and broods entertainingly. He manages to extract a lot of gloomy introspection from a place where I have always had rather jolly holidays. No mean feat.

Touching the Void by Joe Simpson (Vintage). My wife complained about me reading this book in bed because of my loud groaning. Mr Simpson climbs up a mountain in Peru, breaks a knee then falls into a crevasse. His account of his agonised crawl to safety may induce involuntary vocal exhalation.

Stalingrad by Anthony Beevor (Viking). Snipcock or possibly Tweed was shown hiding a John Grisham under the dust cover of this book in a Private Eye cartoon. Poor man. I have never read a more gripping account of human folly and the ghastliness of battle. I would rather be run over by a T34 than read John Grisham.

City of the World's Desire by Philip Mansel (Penguin). This is a sparkling, unputdownable history book. It tells the story of Istanbul and forced me to ditch every received opinion I had formerly entertained about the sick man of Europe. This is history with people as people, not statistics.

Are You Experienced? by William Sutcliffe (Penguin). A first-class comic novel about a year out on the Hippy trail. Not as dark, jagged and mysterious as The Beach by Alex Garland, but undoubtedly more true.

145

Andrew Roberts

*Author and historian Andrew Roberts chooses his six favourite histories and biographies, both published and forthcoming. His book, **Napoleon and Wellington**, is published by Weidenfeld.*

Issue 345: 16th February 2002

Daydream Believer by Hugh Massingberd (Macmillan). This autobiography is one of the few books of the past decade that I would label sublime. Massingberd's disarming honesty about himself and the mixture of romance, snobbery and love of history that actuates him is told with modesty and wit.

Berlin: the Downfall, 1945 by Antony Beevor (Viking). If this book has half the pace and scholarship of Stalingrad, it will be superb. Beevor has discovered some terrible truths about the "liberation" of Eastern Europe, including the revelation that the Red Army raped some six million women along the way.

Diplomacy and Murder in Teheran by Laurence Kelly (IB Tauris). This excellent book is the story of a young aristocratic Russian intellectual and playwright, and his terrible death along with the rest of the Russian legation in Teheran in 1829.

How To Lose Friends and Alienate People by Toby Young (Little, Brown). A masterpiece about Young's experiences working for Vanity Fair in New York that made me laugh out loud. Young has made himself the anti-hero of the book, yet by the end the reader is hoping he will succeed, knowing he won't, and despising the criteria that New York sets for success anyhow.

Jeremy Thorpe by Michael Bloch (Little, Brown). This controversial biography has revelations and good writing in equal measure. Two decades after Thorpe's trial, it is now possible to bring objectivity to those weird and extraordinary events.

Victor, Third Baron Rothschild by Kenneth Rose (Weidenfeld & Nicolson). Every work that Rose has produced, such as Superior Person (the life of Lord Curzon) and King George V, has been a work of art; this life of his friend, the late Lord Rothschild, is no exception.

Anthony Sampson

Anthony Sampson, author and journalist, chooses six recent books which have changed his view of contemporary history. His own book, **Mandela, the Authorised Biography***, is published by HarperCollins.*

Issue 259: 10th June 2000

King Leopold's Ghost by Adam Hochschild (Macmillan) is the scholarly and dramatic story of the Belgian slave-empire in the Congo, written with a deep knowledge of Africa, which is intensely relevant to the continent today – including vivid portraits of villains and crusaders, from King Leopold and Stanley to Casement and Conrad.

The Langhorne Sisters by James Fox (Granta) is a brilliant account of how a family of Southern Belles from Virginia married into great wealth and became part of a unique Anglo-American network of influence, headed by the Astors. It's more readable than any Forsyth Saga or Buddenbrooks, written with the sensitivity of a descendant.

Who Paid the Piper? by Helen Stonor Saunders (Granta) uncovers the secret bargains behind the CIA's financing of European cultural institutions and organisations like Encounter magazine, with fascinating insights into intellectuals including Stephen Spender, Melvin Lasky and Malcolm Muggeridge.

John Major, the Autobiography (HarperCollins) is an indispensable and surprisingly compelling account of a remarkable political career, much more revealing than Thatcher's memoir, with sharp sideswipes at his treacherous colleagues, "The Bastards". And he wrote it himself.

The Letters of Kingsley Amis (HarperCollins) are often even funnier than his novels, displaying all the weaknesses, vulnerabilities and ultimate undoing of its central character with a candour which is thoroughly disarming.

White Teeth by Zadie Smith (Hamish Hamilton) is a novel, but it gave me a more convincing picture of multi-racial life in London than any report. It is funny, unsentimental and unpredictable, with dialogue which seems made for the TV series which it is to become.

Andrew Samuels

Andrew Samuels is a Jungian analyst, academic and writer. His book, the award-winning **Politics on the Couch: Citizenship and the Internal Life,** *is published by Karnac.*

Issue 460: 15th May 2004

Memories, Dreams, Reflections by Carl Gustav Jung (Fontana Press). Not really an autobiography, more an account of how the internal life unfolds in tandem with external events. Still one of the best ways to encounter Jung's thought. His account of his dreams and how he came to understand them is gripping.

For Whom the Bell Tolls by Ernest Hemingway (Arrow). This was the book that introduced me to female desire when I was an adolescent. The love of Maria for Robert Jordan struck me as impossible at first, yet gradually I saw how a woman might have similar experiences and anxieties to my own.

Constantine's Sword by James Carroll (Houghton Mifflin). The best account of the origins of anti-Semitism that I have found. He shows how the development within Christianity of the idea that it had superseded Judaism led inevitably to a need to destroy the older religion.

Venice by James Morris (Faber). This is the travel book I most remember. Morris intersperses the big picture with little details every inch of the way. Highlights include Robert Benchley of The New Yorker cabling on arrival: "Streets full of water, please advise" and a grave-stone inscription: "Major X, left us in peace May 23rd 1889".

Book of Ecclesiastes, Old Testament. The cautionary tale of all times and more relevant than ever in an age of global terrorism – "the sound of the grinding is low and then mourners go about the streets". The source of old-fashioned idealism about working out what really matters in life.

Cheri and The Last of Cheri by Colette (Vintage). Another autobiographical choice – about the transgressive aspects of love across the generations under the radar of the thought police. The love affair between the courtesan Leah and Cheri is one the most beautiful tales of amorality in fiction.

148

Jeremy Scott

Writer and bon viveur Jeremy Scott chooses his six favourite books.
*His autobiography, **Fast and Louche**, is published by Profile Books.*

Issue 426: 13th September 2003

Meditations of Marcus Aurelius (Penguin) The 2nd century Roman emperor wrote the world's first self-help book and, unlike his imitators, didn't do so to make money. In it he describes how to achieve freedom, peace, happiness, and change your life. During a total reversal of fortune a while ago he literally saved my own.

Four Quartets by T.S. Eliot (Faber & Faber) Montaigne observes that in reading we retain nothing, we cannot say we know a book unless it has changed us. Eliot did it for me: at the age of 15, I found his verse incantatory, a spell by which I could plug into a spiritual dimension.

Greenmantle by John Buchan (Oxford University Press) Buchan writes about a world where men were men and the women they fell in love with had slim hips and looked like boys and were jolly brave too. These chaps enjoyed a private income, travelled lots and had adventures; aged 12 it looked like the life for me.

Brideshead Revisited by Evelyn Waugh (Penguin) Flawless social observation, wit and tragedy. The novel elegiacally evokes a world of reckless, selfish people, which in adolescence struck me as infinitely glamorous. I longed to be behaving badly with the worst of them.

Goncourt Journals by Edmond and Jules de Goncourt (Out of print) The brothers led an intensely social life; their joint diary covers Paris during the period 1851-96. A clinical dissection of literary, artistic and theatrical milieus; anecdotes, scandal and gossip. Recognisably like today, but more fun.

Essays of William Hazlitt (Blackwell) A needy, quarrelsome hack, but goodness how one warms to him! Whatever the topic, he writes of the whole human condition. His essay On the Want of Money (a situation that he, like myself, found all too familiar) is wonderfully heartening.

Will Self

*Author and journalist Will Self chooses his six favourite literary biographies. His novel, **How the Dead Live**, is published by Bloomsbury and was shortlisted for the Whitbread Novel of the Year Award.*

Issue 288: 6th January 2001

Oscar Wilde by Richard Elman (Out of print). Despite the fact that Mervyn Holland, the writer's grandson, has severe misgivings about it, to my mind Elman's book remains one of the great biographies, literary or otherwise. It gives a flavour of what it must have been like to swap anecdotes with Wilde et al.

Bernard Shaw by Michael Holroyd (Vintage). I particularly relish Holroyd's Borgesian conceit that, on contemplating writing Shaw's life, he calculated that unless he lived to a prodigiously great age, he wouldn't have time to read every word his subject had written. It's surprising how sympathetic Holroyd's Shaw remains, beneath the hideous patina of greatness.

Literary Outlaw: the Life and Times of William S. Burroughs by Ted Morgan (Out of print). The definitive biography of Burroughs. Although allegedly disliked by his subject, Morgan is surprisingly kind to the uxoricidal maniac who, perhaps more than any English-speaking writer, redefined the parameters of what fiction could do in the 20th century. A brilliant insight into the counter-cultural circles in which Burroughs moved.

Coleridge by Richard Holmes (Harper Collins). Deeply sad, deeply moving and piercingly sensual. Holmes doesn't spare Coleridge – the arch procrastinator, the awful plagiarist, the domestic deserter, the hopeless drug addict – but he gives an insight into the man that takes psycho-biography on to a new plane.

Marcel Proust by George Painter (Out of print). Proustian in its conception, full of serpentine sentences and descriptions of flowers. Although superseded by later exegesis, Painter's biography contains the best tips on how to become like the author of À la Recherche.

Blake by Peter Ackroyd (Vintage). Blake lived his entire life within the compass of the city of London (it's worth remembering that the "dark satanic mills" of "Jerusalem" were sited on the Farringdon Road). Ackroyd's recreation of his milieu is a masterly feat of time travel.

John Sergeant

*John Sergeant, the ex-political editor of ITN, chooses his six favourite books. His memoir, **Give Me Ten Seconds**, is published in paperback by Pan.*

Issue 370: 10th August 2002

The Life of Samuel Johnson by James Boswell (Oxford Paperbacks). Now we are going heavyweight. It's long and there are lots of boring passages, but if you can get through all the verbiage it's the greatest biography ever written. If you want a trip back to the 18th century in the company of the most brilliant man of his time, this is it.

Citizens by Simon Schama (Penguin). Long before he became the great TV history man, Schama wrote this marvellous book about the French Revolution. It packs in all the anecdotes and personality you would expect and makes you thankful that you did not have to live through those times.

Down and Out in Paris and London by George Orwell (Penguin). Perhaps the greatest writer of English prose in the 20th century, Orwell taught my generation how to write and how to think. I thought the selection of this book in particular would provide a useful antidote to my last choice.

The Good Food Guide (Which? Books). Well, you can't spend all your time reading. But you will need sufficient funds to check on the accuracy of their research. It's surprising, though, how often in fancy restaurants (and usually I'm not paying) I see people who are not amazingly rich. They are just very keen on good food.

Three Men in a Boat by Jerome K. Jerome (Penguin). A comedy classic, which is still wonderfully funny. Pointless activity, seriously undertaken, is the stuff of sailing holidays. This book explains why people like me can't resist playing captain and crew each summer; and why, despite all our efforts, it can easily degenerate into farce.

Scoop by Evelyn Waugh (Penguin). A bit dated and not at all politically correct, but this remains the best satire on the hopeless attempts by journalists to whip up interest in obscure wars. All his more ludicrous inventions I can now vouch for as being true.

151

Gerald Seymour

*Gerald Seymour, the author of 17 bestselling novels including **Harry's Game** and **The Glory Boys**, chooses his six favourite books. His book, **Holding the Zero**, is published by Bantam.*

Issue 239: 22nd January 2000

Most Secret by Nevil Shute (Out of print). My favourite contemporary WWII novel. Shute's craft is an inspiration to me. The story of occupied France, the nobility of resistance and personal sacrifice, allow me to walk with fiction's finest heroes – usually with a wet eye.

The Unlikely Spy by Paul Henderson (Macmillan). An extraordinary picture of the nightmare life of a British intelligence agent. Henderson gave MI6 a view into Iraq's military superstructure and if caught would have gone to a Baghdad gallows; his reward was to be abandoned by our spymasters and politicians. Edge-of-the-seat stuff.

Ivanhoe by Walter Scott (Oxford University Press). One of the greatest adventure stories of the English language and responsible – thank God – for driving myriads of pimpled teenage youths (me included) into the worlds of books, fantasies, imagination and enthusiasm. Epic and unmatched storytelling.

Natasha's Story by Michael Nicholson (Macmillan). More than just a wonderful love story of how a feisty orphan was plucked from besieged Sarajevo and brought to England – while the huge majority of us were wringing our hands and doing nothing – but also a brilliantly drawn sketch of that tragic city.

The Domesday Book of Mammoth Pike by Fred Buller (Stanley Paul, out of print). A classic for obsessionalist pike anglers and required reading for anyone setting out for a frozen river bank in search of these leviathan predators – supreme escapism from a dreary world.

Carling's England by Barry Newcombe (Harvill). I love the ethos and culture of old rugby. Unsettled by the bankruptcy of the modern English game, I take comfort from returning to this tale of the eccentrics and characters who wore the white shirt a decade ago – we won't see their like again.

Ned Sherrin

*Ned Sherrin, the producer, director, author and presenter of Radio 4's Loose Ends, chooses his six favourite humorous books. His novel, **Scratch an Actor**, is published by Mandarin.*

Issue 196: 20th March 1999

No Bed for Bacon by Caryl Brahms and S.J. Simon. (Black Swan). Reprinted as a result of the fuss made by fans who saw similarities with Shakespeare in Love (both involve Shakespeare, Elizabeth I and a lady in waiting who dresses up as a boy). No Bed... and Don't, Mr Disraeli started a vogue for anachronistic historical fiction like Blackadder.

Scoop by Evelyn Waugh (Penguin). As with Brahms and Simon I could name half-a-dozen Waugh novels, but this one must stand for them all. It features an omnipotent press magnate, Lord Copper, and the memorable catch phrase: "Up to a point, Lord Copper..."

A Bullet in the Ballet by Caryl Brahms and S.J. Simon (Civers Press). The first of a hilarious series of novels blissfully sending up the touring Russian ballet companies of the Twenties, Thirties and Forties. Great comic characters led by the impresario Stroganoff and Nevajno, "choreographer of the future", with his perpetual plea: "You schange schmall scheque?"

Nicholas Nickleby by Charles Dickens (Penguin). The story of a generous, high-spirited lad, especially memorable for the immortal Vincent Crummles touring theatre company.

The Inimitable Jeeves by P.G. Wodehouse (Century). Again a standard bearer for a whole shelf of Bertie Wooster novels – elegant, stylish and above all funny.

Valmouth by Ronald Firbank (Wordsworth). This exquisite, camp novel, set in a watering place dominated by the erotic black masseuse Mrs Yajñavalkya, was amazingly well-realised by Sandy Wilson in his musical version, which also plundered a character from Firbank's Concerning the Eccentricities of Cardinal Pirelli.

Clare Short

Clare Short MP chooses her six favourite recent reads. Her own book,
An Honourable Deception? New Labour, Iraq and the Misuse of Power,
is published by Simon & Schuster.

Issue 499: 19th Feb 2005

High Noon: 20 Global Problems, 20 Years to Solve Them by J.E. Rischard (Perseus Press). Rischard, the World Bank's vice-president for Europe, catalogues the 20 most important global problems we have to solve. This book helps us to rise above the trivialisation of modern politics and face the challenges of our age.

I Didn't Do it For You: How the World Betrayed a Small African Nation by Michela Wrong (HarperCollins). Wrong's second book on Africa tells the story of Eritrea, from Mussolini's dreams of a new Roman Empire to the war with Ethiopia. It's a wonderful read, and a reminder of why Africa is in its current state.

Dining with Terrorists: Meeting with the World's Most Wanted Militants by Phil Rees (Macmillan). This highly readable account of the people involved in the movements now branded as "terrorism" offers a deep understanding of the conditions that generate violent resistance and offers suggestions on how to put things right.

Small Island by Andrea Levy (Headline). A beautiful novel – and this year's Whitbread winner – about Jamaican servicemen coming to help the mother country during the Second World War. It makes us face the cruelty of racism, but also shows the generosity of the human spirit.

Imperial Hubris: Why the West is Losing the War on Terror by Anonymous (Brassey's Inc). Anonymous, who has been outed as a senior CIA analyst, gives insight into the mind of Osama bin Laden. We learn that bin Laden sincerely loves his God, does not hate us because he hates freedom, and has a rational, long-term plan to change the situation in the Middle East.

A History of God by Karen Armstrong (Vintage). This book describes the way in which Judaism, Christianity and Islam have strongly influenced each other, and explodes once and for all the idea of a clash of civilisations.

Gillian Slovo

*Author Gillian Slovo chooses her six favourite novels. Her play **Guantanamo** received critical acclaim, while her novel, **Ice Road**, was shortlisted for the Orange Prize.*

Issue 503: 19th March 2005

The Plot Against America by Philip Roth (Vintage).Roth rewrites American history, replacing Roosevelt in the White House with Nazi sympathiser Charles Lindbergh. The novel has all the clarity and inventiveness of Roth's prose, combined with a new gentleness, and says as much about America's possible future as it does about its recent past.

Bleak House by Charles Dickens (Penguin). Dickens's effortless, complicated, elegant and moving story set against the backdrop of the court case of Jarndyce v Jarndyce. A knock-out blow to inequality and the pomposity of the law, without sacrificing the integrity of its characters.

Slaughterhouse 5 by Kurt Vonnegut (Vintage). A time traveller in the midst of war. This is a passionate and funny novel about the Allied fire bombing of Dresden that brings all Vonnegut's wacky imagination to bear on the issues of the barbarity of war and of our common humanity.

She Came to Stay by Simone de Beauvoir (HarperCollins). A ménage à trois set in a Paris soon to fall to the Germans. A novel about passion, politics and revenge that is told with a breathtaking clarity and directness. No-holds-barred writing that epitomises Simone de Beauvoir's before-her-time boldness.

Anna Karenina by Leo Tolstoy (Penguin). That most fated of love affairs told by a writer who is equally at home when describing a frock, a death or a religo-philosophical dilemma. Virtuoso storytelling of characters whose credibility lies in their often fatal flaws.

History by Elsa Morante (Penguin). A hugely ambitious epic that traces the lives of ordinary people – in particular a mother and her passion for the son born out of her rape by a German soldier – who are trying to survive in war-torn Italy. A buried treasure that sometimes takes persistence, but ultimately delivers.

Jon Snow

Jon Snow, presenter of Channel 4 News and Weekly Planet, selects the six books that most influenced him during different stages of his life.

Issue 118: 6th September 1997

The Children of the New Forest by Captain Marryat (Penguin). Stirring tale about a family of orphaned Royalist children who flee into the New Forest to escape the Cromwellians. Can I really have been such a Monarchist as to have loved this at nine years old? But I did, not least the children's magnificent self-sufficiency.

Alan Clark's Diaries (Harper Collins). For anyone confronting authority on a daily basis – a teacher's aid. His admission of a desire to pee on the populace from his eighth-floor office on his first day as a Minister invades the humbug that shrouds so much of public life.

Bonfire of the Vanities by Tom Wolfe (Pan). The novel of the venal aspect of the 1980s, signalled what was to become of the "me first" brigade. A seminal impact even in my 40s.

Angela's Ashes by Frank McCourt (Harper Collins). A wondrous and assaulting insight into the survival of great suffering in childhood: an epic, read this summer, that reaches far beyond Empire's poison, Catholicism and the Ireland in which it is set.

Three Men in a Boat by Jerome K Jerome (Penguin). I was especially taken by Uncle Bodger's attempts to hang pictures – loved and laughed aloud when reading it at the age of 12.

Sons and Lovers by DH Lawrence (Penguin). Whoever set this for A-level English in 1966 needs a medal. Forced to read it at the age at which I was most vulnerable to its passion. Come back Miriam, all is forgiven!

David Stafford

*Author David Stafford selects five of the best books about the Special Operations Executive. His book, **Secret Agent**, accompanied the BBC2 television series.*

Issue 267: 5th August 2000

Foreign Fields by Peter Wilkinson (IB Tauris). Wilkinson supplied weapons to the Czech agents who assassinated SS chief Reinhard Heydrich. This autobiography vividly captures the Eric Ambler world of Thirties central Europe and the hardships of Wilkinson's own wartime mission into Austria.

Flames in the Field by Rita Kramer (Out of print). Shortly after D-Day four female SOE agents were murdered in Struthof-Natzweiler concentration camp. Were they deliberately betrayed in a campaign of Allied deception? Kramer speculates intelligently and it's impossible not to be moved by this unsentimental account.

SOE in France by M.R.D. Foot (Out of print). The first official history of SOE. A masochist's delight, with its 500 densely written pages. But the gain is worth the pain. It remains unmatched in its mastery of SOE operational detail.

Skis Against the Atom by Knut Haukelid (Out of print). This is the account of how the SOE agents frustrated Nazi plans to build the atom bomb by sabotaging the heavy water plant in Norway. Only Norwegians had the toughness to operate in this climate and it had all the hallmarks of a suicide mission. Told by one of the participants, it's an epic tale.

The Killing of SS Obergruppenführer Reinhard Heydrich by Callum MacDonald (Macmillan). The best account of any SOE operation. A skilfully crafted book, it weaves together operational and political strands into a compelling narrative. Hard to beat as an illustration of the harsh realpolitik that underpins the world of secret intelligence.

Peter Stothard

Peter Stothard, editor of the TLS, former editor of The Times and author of **Thirty Days: A Month at the Heart of Blair's War** (Harper Collins), chooses his five favourite books.

Issue 506: 9th April 2005

The Satires, Book One by Horace (Penguin). An early primer for political journalists. The poet takes a stomach-churning road-and-canal trip with powerful friends, peace-making between the future Emperor Augustus and rival Roman warlords. Satire Five, the Journey to Brundisium, provides a vivid personal picture of the man who created European literature – and descriptions of place that influenced millions of newspaper writers, whether they know it or not.

The Secret History by Procopius (Penguin). The Emperor Justinian had an historian who wrote three very different works, the first a critical account of campaigns, the second a sycophantic summary of imperial architecture, the third, The Secret History, a damning kiss-and-tell of (among other things) what the Empress did with her pubic regions, pieces of corn and pet geese. Pornography for learned schoolboys.

The Nun's Priest's Tale by Geoffrey Chaucer (Oxford University Press). An overbearing cockerel learns the vanity of dreams. Any newspaper editor (or anyone else) who is tempted to feel cock of the walk, who is beset by fakes and flatterers and liable to use more Latin quotations than is good for him, needs to read this story from The Canterbury Tales, one of the first and still the funniest in English verse.

The Double Man by W.H. Auden (Out of print). One of the Devil's tricks is to link the truth to a lie, expose the lie, "and so treat babe and bathwater the same". The poet's New York meditation in 1940 on Hitler, history and how even 2,000 years of European civilisation can be readily denied.

Illness as Metaphor by Susan Sontag (Penguin). A critic in 1977 faces up to the cancer that killed her in 2005 and spurs others to do the same. How truth and lies are part of the very disease – and how political propaganda helped to make them so.

Sir Roy Strong

*Sir Roy Strong, historian, writer and broadcaster, chooses six of the best gardening books to read in winter. His book, **The Spirit of Britain – A Narrative History of the Arts**, is published by Pimlico.*

Issue 279: 28th October 2000

The Education of a Gardener by Russell Page (Harvill). Although Page conceals more than he reveals about himself, nonetheless this remains a classic in which, through sharing in his education, we in turn are educated in the principles of good garden design and also in how to look.

The Startling Jungle by Stephen Lacey (Out of print). Reading solidly about plants bores me, but this is a rare book which will make anyone, me included, want to turn the page excitedly to learn, for instance, that the scent of Osmanthus delavayi has the "penetrating smell of cheap suntan lotion".

A Gentle Plea for Chaos by Mirabel Osler (Bloomsbury). A writer in love with language as much as with her garden and its wayward plants which die on her or grow in the wrong direction. Her opinionated idiosyncrasy I find irresistible. This is gardening as a tempestuous, angry love affair.

The Well-Tempered Garden by Christopher Lloyd (Lyons Press). Where would we be without this benign minor national monument? For beginners, it is the most welcoming invitation that I know to step out and not be ashamed to make a fool of yourself in the garden.

The Tulip by Anne Pavord (Bloomsbury). An instant classic from its first appearance. It is the narrative history of a single flower told with both passion and authority.

Onward and Upward in the Garden by Katherine S. White (Ingram). The funniest garden book I know, written by a lady who gardened in her Ferragamo shoes. Essentially a collection of pieces for The New Yorker, it left me shrieking with laughter. Who would ever think that seed catalogues could be hilarious?

Alan Titchmarsh

*Alan Titchmarsh, the gardener, author and presenter of the BBC's Gardener's World and Ground Force, chooses his six favourite books. His third novel, **Animal Instincts**, is published by Simon & Schuster.*

Issue 283: 25th November 2000

Rebecca by Daphne du Maurier (Arrow). Du Maurier is a classy yarn-spinner. I first read Rebecca in a shed during a rainy week in the Sixties when I was taking money at the local putting green in Ilkley, Yorkshire. I can still recall the excitement of the story.

Blandings Castle by P.G. Wodehouse (Penguin). Lord Emsworth is one of my favourite characters in fiction and Wodehouse is by far the most skilful comedic writer of the 20th century. To say, for instance, that a cow "lacks sustained dramatic interest" shows great agricultural insight.

Pride and Prejudice by Jane Austen (Penguin). This is one of the funniest books ever written. I love Austen's waspishness and her ability to burst bubbles of pomposity and grandeur so effectively.

Captain Corelli's Mandolin by Louis de Bernières (Minerva). I felt like giving up on this novel – the first few chapters, about the invasion of a Greek island during World War II, are so disconnected. But I'm glad I kept going – it's one of the most rewarding, emotional books I have read in years.

Thérèse Raquin by Emile Zola (Penguin). I don't so much like this book as admire Zola's ability to create an atmosphere – a chilling, sickly one at that. Read it and shudder as passion turns to tragedy.

The Wind in the Willows by Kenneth Grahame (Methuen). I reread this regularly, to escape I suppose. But it reinforces my love of the countryside. Every child should be given it as an antidote to that wretched Pokémon.

Claire Tomalin

The biographer Claire Tomalin chooses six books that make imaginative use of England's historical archives. Her biography, **Samuel Pepys: The Unequalled Self***, won the Whitbread Book of the Year prize.*

Issue 398: 1st March 2003

The Gentleman's Daughter by Amanda Vickery (Yale University Press). Stories of Georgian courtship and marriage – funny, sad, earthy, and all direct from the letters and diaries of the women involved.

Victorian Miniature by Owen Chadwick (Cambridge University Press). A study of the battle between squire and parson in the tiny Norfolk village of Ketteringham, based on diaries kept by both men in the mid-19th century. The result is a narrative worthy of Trollope at his best – but all true.

Life As We Have Known It edited by Margaret Llewelyn Davies (Out of print). A collection of memoirs by very poor women – women whose children routinely died of undernourishment. A chronicle of hardship and almost unbelievably callous usage from their social superiors. It was first published in 1930, and once read, never forgotten.

The Voices of Morebath by Eamon Duffy (Yale University Press). Duffy opens a window into 16th century life in a Devonshire village through the account book of its priest, who nursed it through the cruel changes imposed by Tudor rulers. History is rarely so immediate and moving.

Uncertain Unions: Marriage in England 1660-1753 by Lawrence Stone (Oxford University Press). From legal and church archives, Stone took scores of scabrous stories: bigamy, seduction, clandestine marriage, fortune hunting and blackmail – shamefully lively entertainment.

Transformations of Love: The Friendship of John Evelyn and Margaret Godolphin by Frances Harris. (Oxford University Press). This exquisite new book unravels the truth of a platonic but passionate love affair at the court of Charles II, between a maid of honour and a middle-aged married scholar.

Each of these books is worth taking slowly, pondering and re-reading, for the intrinsic value of the raw material and for the skilful way in which it has been deployed.

Joanna Trollope

Joanna Trollope, the novelist, selects six imagination-stretching books for beginners. "The trouble about prescriptive reading lists is that they invite resentment – I shall nurse mine about Pope's Dunciad to the grave."

Photo: Véronique Rolland

Issue 79: 30th November 1996

The Wyrd Sisters by Terry Pratchett (Corgi). Here be jokes. Real, witty quirky jokes plus the bonus of a sideways take on Shakespeare which might just send one child scurrying for Lambs' Tales…

The Bird of Dawning by John Masefield (Out of print). Something everyone likes sometimes – a proper story, full of adventure and sea-going detail. It's the tale of the annual race of 19th-century tea clippers home from China and there isn't a soppy line in it.

The Dark is Rising by Susan Cooper (Penguin). A compelling read with Tolkien-like concerns about our dark and ancient roots. Easy language, huge ideas.

Treasure Island by R.L. Stevenson (Penguin). Among all its other riches, this has the purest, most hypnotic dose of fear-on-the-page – blind Pugh and his tapping stick on the lonely, empty road.

I Capture the Castle by Dodie Smith (Arrow). Family life and first love seen through the sharp eyes of adolescent Cassandra. Next stop, Pride and Prejudice?

The Wind in the Willows by Kenneth Graham (Penguin). A matchless introduction to the possibilities of metaphor, plus comedy and lyricism and, of course, the abiding lure of furry things.

Lynne Truss

*Lynne Truss, the writer and broadcaster, chooses her six favourite comic novels. Her book, **Eats, Shoots & Leaves: The Zero Tolerance Approach to Punctuation**, is published by Profile Books.*

Issue 442: 10th January 2004

The Code of the Woosters by P.G. Wodehouse (Penguin). A perfect Jeeves novel, this is the one with the cow creamer, in which Bertie travels to Totleigh Towers with nefarious intent and falls foul of the sappy Madeline Bassett. Classic and wonderful stuff.

The Ascent of Rum Doodle by W.E. Bowman (Pimlico). First published in 1956, this is that rare beast: a mountaineering spoof. The tone is that of Three Men in a Boat; the context is Everest; the punchline is "We had climbed the wrong mountain". Team member Tom Burley succumbs to every kind of lassitude imaginable: heat lassitude, valley lassitude, glacier lassitude.

Molesworth by Geoffrey Willans and Ronald Searle (Penguin). A one-volume edition of the great Molesworth books of the Fifties. Like Wodehouse, Molesworth uses American slang to fantastic effect. But the best things in Molesworth are the sound effects, WAM PLUNK BISH BASH ZUNK.

The Trick of It by Michael Frayn (Faber & Faber). A highly sophisticated comic novel about an academic who marries the woman novelist whose work he has admired. Once married, he undermines her fatally. A novel about talent, jealousy and the fatal vulnerability of creative people, it is funny, painful, superb.

Diary of a Nobody by George and Weedon Grossmith (Penguin). The faux naif narrator is now a very well-established strain of English comic writing, yet the diary of Charles Pooter remains fresh and funny to this day.

Barchester Towers by Anthony Trollope (Oxford University Press). Studying Barchester Towers for A-level, I managed not to notice that it's hilarious. I now regard it as the pinnacle of English comic writing. Published in 1857, the second of the Barsetshire Chronicles, it's a story of virtue versus ambition in the context of High Victorian church, politics and journalism.

Ed Victor

Ed Victor, literary agent and vice-chairman of the Almeida Theatre, chooses a favourite book from each decade of his life.

Issue 202: 1st May 1999

1940s – The Naked and the Dead by Norman Mailer (Paladin). To my mind, this is the greatest of all war novels. When, suddenly, in the middle of the book, the young lieutenant is killed by a Japanese bullet, my heart almost stopped. Amazing that Mailer went to war in order to write "the great American novel"... and then did.

1950s – The Catcher in the Rye by J.D. Salinger (Penguin). Without question, the finest example of a novel about growing up I have ever read. It captures all the joys and agonies of adolescence, especially of the male variety. When I read it, as a young teenager, I was shocked that somebody truly understood what I was going through.

1960s – Catch 22 by Joseph Heller (Vintage). Its sheer inventiveness puts this book in a class of its own. It remains a breathtaking excursion into the madness in the marrow of our bones.

1970s – 100 Years of Solitude by Gabriel Garcia Marquez (Penguin). An astonishing kaleidoscope of a novel, taking the reader on the literary trip of a lifetime. I once heard someone at a dinner party ask Marquez what drugs he was taking while he was writing 100 Years. "Drugs?" he asked, "100 years is not the product of drugs. In my country it is considered socialist realism."

1980s – The Bonfire of the Vanities by Tom Wolfe (Picador). The very definition of the Eighties. Wolfe is a great satirist, to be compared with Swift or Thackeray. Just as people turn to Jane Austen to comprehend English life in the early 19th century, Wolfe will deliver late 20th century America to readers of the future.

1990s – The Reader by Bernhard Schlink (Phoenix House). A bleak, austere and gripping attempt to make us think about the unthinkable: the Holocaust. Brilliantly translated by Carol Janeway, it has the dark power of a Grimm fairy tale, and, in its apparent simplicity, poses the most complicated questions in the mind of the reader.

Terry Waite

*Terry Waite chooses six memorable books he read during his four years in captivity. In the first 12 months he received no books. "Eventually, a kindly guard promised to bring me some. One of his first offerings, **A Manual of Breast Feeding**, would not qualify for my list."*

Issue 182: 5th December 1998

A Pattern of Islands by Arthur Grimble (Ulverscroft). A splendid account of colonial administration in the Gilbert and Ellis Islands. I remembered these islands because as a boy their distinctive postage stamps found a place in my album. Grimble was a great and humorous administrator. Essential reading for Robin Cook!

History of the Greek and Persian War by Herodotus (Penguin). The writer brought a bit of historical gossip into my cell. The fact that it was ancient gossip made no difference. I had no watch, no radio, and didn't even know the date!

A Tree Grows in Brooklyn by Betty Smith (Mandarin). An American classic that ought to be read more widely over here. Wonderful descriptions of a New York childhood by an Irish immigrant.

As I Walked Out One Midsummer Morning by Laurie Lee (Penguin). Enchanting account of Lee's travels across Spain. If only I could have walked out any morning! A poetic read and a book to curl up with on a winter's night.

Busman's Honeymoon by Dorothy L. Sayers (BBC). When it comes to detective novels DLS leaves Agatha Christie at the bus stop. Splendid characters of whom the like can still be found in remote parts of Essex and Suffolk. Witty erudite.

The Brothers Karamazov by Dostoyevsky (Penguin). A tale involving anarchism, atheism and the existence of God. Just the stuff for a good solitary read.

Simon Ward

The actor Simon Ward, who shot to fame playing Churchill in Young Winston, chooses his five favourite books. He also reviews books for The Spectator and the Literary Review.

Issue 354: 20th April 2002

The Complete Essays by Michel de Montaigne (Penguin). I discovered Montaigne – the 16th century moralist and essayist – some ten years ago and I dip into him every day. On his retirement at 40 Montaigne locked himself away in his library to muse on, well, everything really, and to share his ponderings with the world. He forms a unique bridge between the classical world and our own.

Evelyn Waugh remains for me the sublime stylist of the last century, but I pick instead **Will This Do?** (House of Strauss), the funny and sometimes terrifying autobiography of his son Auberon, partly doing so to punish the father for so greedily eating all Bron's bananas.

Negotiate the first chapter of Patrick O'Brian's **Master and Commander** (HarperCollins) and an ocean of excitement opens before you. This book is the first of 20 adventures featuring Captain Aubrey and Dr Maturin as they do battle with the Napoleonic navy. Travel, fighting, history and the most exquisitely believable love between two fighting men.

I first read **Night Life of the Gods** by Thorne Smith (Random House) when I was 12 and again a whole series of wonderment was revealed, only in this case comic and extraordinary. Smith died young and is almost forgotten, but his tales of invisibility and sexy ghosts, of statues of randy gods escaping from the Metropolitan Museum have always entranced me – possibly because Smith's heroes are always shy, innocent young men pursued by luscious ladies.

Finally an oddity: **Arctic Dreams** by Barry Lopez (Harvill Panther). I know of no better introduction to any strange land than Lopez provides in this hypnotic account of life in the gleaming wastes of the far north. It is geography, history, biology and ecology written with passionate knowledge; every single moment enthralled me.

Marina Warner

*Author and historian Marina Warner selects her favourite fairy tale books. Her book, **No Go the Bogeyman**, about ogres and other figures of fear, is published by Chatto.*

Issue 127: 8th November 1997

Cosmicomix by Italo Calvino (Pan) A brilliant inventor of new fantastic fables (something that's not so easy to do), Calvino is at his very best here, with wildly imaginative tales that create an alternative story for the once-upon-a-time of the world's origins.

The Book of Imaginary Beings by Jorge Luis Borges (Penguin). The master fabulist of them all, Borges gathers together the most effervescent lore about mythical beasts from every kind of source – Chinese mythology to Kafka.

The Complete Short Stories by Angela Carter (Vintage) A wondrous feast of an anthology, including the witty, erotic fairy tales of The Bloody Chamber and later reflections with the unique Carteresque mix of lyricism and gallows humour.

After Ovid New Metamorphoses edited by Michael Hofmann and James Lasdun (Faber). Leading poets – including Paul Muldoon and Ted Hughes – respond to Ovid's great work of mythology with their own versions of the stories.

The Metamorphoses of Antoninus Liberalis, edited by Francis Celoria (Routledge). A new translation of almost unknown Greek legends, with a highly original but very learned commentary on aspects of lore from nightingales to typhoons.

The Arabian Nights: A Companion by Robert Irwin (Allen Lane) Deftly handled account of the history behind Scheherezade's tour de force, by a writer who uniquely combines skills as an Arabist and a novelist.

Mary Warnock

Mary Warnock, philosopher, educationalist and former mistress of Girton College, Cambridge, chooses her six favourite books.
*Her book, **A Memoir: People and Places**, is published by Duckworth.*

Issue 282: 18th November 2000

The Treatise of Human Nature by David Hume (Oxford University Press). One of the greatest of all philosophical works, covering knowledge, imagination, emotion, morality and justice. Hume is down-to-earth, capable of putting other, pretentious philosophers down, but deeply sceptical even about his own reasoning.

The Prelude by William Wordsworth (Penguin). The idea of a poetic autobiography is to me intensely interesting; and so is the connecting of memory, imagination and place. The account of a young man's excitement at the beginning of the French Revolution is immediate history. The whole great poem is a moving unity.

Coleridge: Darker Reflections by Richard Holmes (HarperCollins). This is the second volume of Holmes's superb biography of Coleridge. It compels one to a rereading of Coleridge's poetry and prose, and to a deeper understanding of the nature of Romantic imagination.

Far Away and Long Ago by W.H. Hudson (Eland). Sharpness of memory and an unfailing eye for natural objects make this one of the greatest accounts of a childhood. Hudson makes one see, and feel, what he sees and feels, even though the South American pampas where he was born is so unfamiliar.

Phineas Finn by Anthony Trollope (Penguin Books). The best of Trollope's political novels. The hero is one of his most engaging Irishmen, ambitious and sexually irresistible. The account of Finn's attempts to make his maiden speech is unforgettable.

Emma by Jane Austen (Penguin). This novel has not only the wit and truth to life of all Austen's novels, but has a deeply sympathetic yet flawed heroine.

Keith Waterhouse

*The author and journalist Keith Waterhouse chooses six of his favourite books. His novel, **Good Grief**, is published by Sceptre.*

Issue 131: 6th December 1997

The Diary of a Provincial Lady by E. M. Delafield (Virago Modern Classics) is worth reading in tandem with the above. This affectionate picture of a middle-class young mother in the Thirties and Forties could not be more in contrast. An entertaining time-warp journey.

The Diary of a Nobody by George and Weedon Grossmith (Penguin) The famous chronicle of the Pooters is the funniest of them all. I have given enough copies of this Victorian classic to keep a small publisher in business, and I still re-read it once a year.

The Penguin Complete Novels of George Orwell From Animal Farm to Nineteen Eighty Four, with the lesser novels – Burmese Days, A Clergyman's Daughter, Coming Up For Air and Keep The Aspidistra Flying – sandwiched in between. One for the desert island.

A Motley Wisdom: The Best of G. K. Chesterton (Hodder & Stoughton). A sampler of the now-neglected polymath: two Father Brown stories, The Man Who Was Thursday, a bit of autobiography, some essays and 15 poems, including The Donkey. Leaves the reader panting for more.

Up In The Old Hotel by Joseph Mitchell (Vintage Books) Definitive collection of the New Yorker's best-ever reporter. Contains McSorley's Wonderful Saloon, about the celebrated though unpretentious Bowery bar that is still going strong.

Bridget Jones's Diary by Helen Fielding (Picador) is, as everyone knows, the runaway bestseller recounting the misadventures of the kind of thirtysomething woman you see whooping it up with her girl-friends in the Café Rouge. A hoot.

Samantha Weinberg

Samantha Weinberg chooses her six favourite books about murder and crime detection. Her book, **Pointing From the Grave – A True Story of Murder and DNA**, *is published by Hamish Hamilton.*

Issue 399: 8th March 2003

The Moonstone by Wilkie Collins (Penguin). One of the first, but still one of the best. A fabulously valuable diamond is stolen from a country house in the 1840s. A series of narrators – from the inspired Sergeant Cuff to the proselytising Drusilla Clack – take us through curses, quick-sands and Indian juggling to a satisfying twist of a solution.

Sidetracked by Henning Mankell (Vintage). My new favourite detective, Inspector Kurt Wallander, lives in a small Swedish town plagued by the most grisly of crimes. In this book, Wallander, dry-humoured and sleep-deprived as ever, tracks down a serial killer with a scalping fixation.

The Talented Mr Ripley by Patricia Highsmith (Vintage).
I remember staying up all night, terrified, to finish this first of the Ripley series. Tom Ripley, a sociopathic liar, kills the friend he admires and steals his identity.

The No.1 Ladies' Detective Agency by Alexander McCall Smith (Polygon). Precious Ramotswe, a Botswana lady built along "traditional lines", founds Gaborone's first detective agency. Using female wisdom and uncommon sense, she solves a series of crimes (husbands eaten by crocodiles, missing children) at the same time affording us a window into the – all too often ignored – beauty, pride and innocence of Africa.

In Cold Blood by Truman Capote (Penguin). A vivid recreation of a murder in the vast plains of middle America. In flawless prose, more novelistic than non-fiction, Capote gets under the skin of the two feckless mur-derers, proving that life can be not only stranger than fiction, but more compelling too.

My Dark Places by James Ellroy (Arrow). Forty years after his mother's unsolved murder, the author of LA Confidential returns to LA to try to find her killer, and in the process – ultimately unsatisfying – reveals his own disturbing secrets. A harrowing but brilliant book.

Fay Weldon

*Author and screenwriter Fay Weldon published her autobiography **Auto la Fay** in 2002 and has since written several more novels*

Issue 304: 28th April 2001

The trouble with best books is that, like best friends, they tend to shift and change in precedence from year to year. And it rather depends on whom you talked to, or read, last. But currently these are the ones surfacing.

Cold Comfort Farm by Stella Gibbons (Penguin). This is a riot of a book that punctured the then-deep seriousness of the English novel, and made writers cautious thereafter, perhaps overcautious, lest they were too earnest and made fools of themselves.

Independent People by Haldor Laxness (Ingram). It is mostly on the strength of this novel that this Icelandic writer won the Nobel Prize for literature in the Fifties. It has the sweep of a Russian novel, the elegance of a French one, and the readability of a book from Britain.

1984 by George Orwell (Penguin). Orwell took things seriously when others didn't, and produced his alarming prophecy of things to come. If society follows art, rather than vice versa, it is Orwell's fault that we now live in the world of double-speak, state enemies who change overnight, and Big Brother.

Brave New World by Aldous Huxley (HarperCollins). Companion piece to the above, Huxley's vision of the future involves a tranquillised society devoted to hygiene, appalled by motherhood and pressured through education into total conformity. This too, paradoxically, was to come about.

Do the **King James' Bible** (Oxford University Press) and **Shakespeare's Sonnets** (BBC) count as "books"? It seems rather a limp description for these pillars of English and indeed world literature. The first provides us, at the very least, with a history of ideas, in unequalled language, the second with a model of what language, properly contrived, metred and rhymed, can do to extend our sensibilities. Not a word, not a thought, wasted. Awesome, as Bridget Jones would say.

Francis Wheen

*Francis Wheen has written about the lives of Tom Driberg and Karl Marx. His book, **Who Was Dr Charlotte Bach?**, is the story of a transvestite philosopher-conman. Here he chooses his favourite books about rogues and rebels.*

Issue 377: 28th September 2002

The Hermit of Peking by Hugh Trevor-Roper (Eland Books). The riveting tale of how Trevor-Roper discovered that the distinguished sinologist Sir Edmund Backhouse was in fact an outrageous forger and swindler.

Giordano Bruno and the Embassy Affair by John Bossy (Yale). "Henry Fagot" was the codename of a secret agent at the French embassy in London who monitored plots and intrigues for Queen Elizabeth I. More than four centuries later, Professor Bossy sensationally identifies the mole as the famous Renaissance philosopher Giordano Bruno.

The Quest for Corvo by A.J.A. Symons (New York Review). Published in 1934, Symons's search for the truth about Baron Corvo pioneered the genre of biography-as-detective-story. It also showed that the lives of rascals and failures are usually more interesting than those of "great men".

A Little Nut-Brown Man by C.M. Vines (Out of print). A.J.P. Taylor, who wrote the official biography of Lord Beaverbrook, said that anyone wanting to know what the old monster was really like should read this gloriously Pooterish account by his former secretary. A comedy classic.

Brewer's Rogues, Villains, Eccentrics: An A-Z of Roguish Britons Through the Ages by William Donaldson (Cassell). This new 660-page encyclopaedia is the funniest book of the year, and quite possibly of all time. Read too much at one sitting and you may have a fatal choking fit. Still, at least you'll die happy.

That Devil Wilkes by Raymond Postgate (Penguin). Postgate, himself a radical bon vivant, was the ideal biographer for John Wilkes, the rakish trouble-maker who sacrificed his own liberty in the cause of free speech.

Katharine Whitehorn

Katharine Whitehorn, journalist, broadcaster and agony aunt for Saga magazine, here chooses six books that have radically changed her thinking.

Issue 149: 18th April 1998

Seeds of Change by Harry Hobhouse (Macmillan). Forget about heroes and ideologies – what really changes the world are such things as quinine, cotton, tea and sugar, and how societies and populations react to their need for them. An eye-opener.

In a Different Voice by Carol Gilligan (Harvard). One of the most penetrating texts of the women's movement, exploding the unconscious assumption of most psychology and ethical theories; that, if women think differently, it must be inferior thinking.

The Driving Force by Michael Crawford and David Marsh (Out of print). The chemical basis of evolution – for example, it's no good the giraffe growing a long neck if its stomach can't digest the higher leaves.

The Blind Watchmaker by Richard Dawkins (Penguin) Brilliant explanation of evolution that takes care of most of the improbabilities. It doesn't prove what he thinks it does – that there is no God – because God is Why, but it's a superb illumination of How.

The Descent of Woman by Elaine Morgan (Souvenir Press). Thanks to Morgan, no one talks about Hunter societies any more – they mention the Gatherers who bring in 65 per cent of the food.

The Economy of Cities by Jane Jacobs (Out of print) How work grows, how cities are not "supported" by the countryside but galvanise it, why grandiose top down schemes don't work and grass-roots do.

The Lit Hit Parade

A number of titles regularly crop as recommendations in The Week's Best Books columns, providing not only a snapshot of the most enduringly popular reads of all time, but also a list of the literary world's favourite authors. As of February 2006, The Week's Literary Hit Parade looks like this.

Position	Votes	
1	14	**Scoop** by Evelyn Waugh **Issues:** 89, 104, 108, 196, 206, 224, 301, 306, 329, 363, 370, 376, 468, 550
2	11	**The Diary of a Nobody** by George and Weedon Grossmith **Issues:** 41, 89, 131, 246, 290, 297, 360, 442, 501, 512, 536
3	9	**Anna Karenina** by Leo Tolstoy **Issues:** 87, 141, 215, 298, 238, 414, 422, 503, 516
4	8	**War and Peace** by Leo Tolstoy **Issues:** 169, 192, 348, 472, 489, 527, 545, 550 **Lucky Jim** by Kingsley Amis **Issues:** 23, 41, 301, 331, 356, 392, 511, 360
5	7	**A La Recherche de Temps Perdu** by Marcel Proust **Issues:** 119, 237, 317, 430, 433, 470, 494 **Jane Eyre** by Charlotte Brontë **Issues:** 25, 148, 189, 195, 308, 407, 422, 508 **The Decline and Fall of the Roman Empire** by Edward Gibbon **Issues:** 125, 207, 329, 433, 440, 481, 470 **The Great Gatsby** by F. Scott Fitzgerald **Issues:** 123, 241, 433, 482, 123, 464, 488 **The Life of Doctor Johnson** by James Boswell **Issues:** 117, 126, 237, 290, 370, 494, 541

Position	Votes	
		Great Expectations by Charles Dickens **Issues:** 85, 163, 238, 273, 290, 365, 492 **Birdsong** by Sebastian Faulks **Issues:** 9, 61, 70, 186, 215, 281, 448 **Ulysses** by James Joyce **Issues:** 25, 90, 99, 181, 185, 212, 229 **Vanity Fair** by William Thackeray **Issues:** 47, 125, 168, 226, 273, 303, 421
6	6	**1984** by George Orwell **Issues:** 304, 310, 351, 405, 492, **Alice's Adventures in Wonderland and Through the Looking-Glass** by Lewis Caroll **Issues:** (3 for Alice: 144, 150, 176 – 2 for the pair: 140 423, 1 for the Looking Glass: 366) **Brideshead Revisited** by Evelyn Waugh **Issues:** 289, 360, 426, 448, 482, 525 **Love in the Time of Cholera** by Gabriel Garcia Marquez **Issues:** 128, 179, 205, 356, 516, 519 **The Leopard** by Giuseppe di Lampedusa **Issues:** 265, 320, 328, 367, 351, 550 **The Wind in the Willows** by Kenneth Graham **Issues:** 79, 193, 283, 338, 383, 384 **Wuthering Heights** by Emily Brontë **Issues:** 192, 230, 374, 396, 405, 423

Position	Votes
7	5
8	4

Pride and Prejudice by Jane Austen
Issues: 4, 148, 176, 215, 348, 283

Catch 22 by Joseph Heller
Issues: 32, 197, 331, 485, 509, 518

Disgrace by J.M. Coetzee
Issues: 413, 428, 443, 476, 487

Emma by Jane Austen
Issues: 123, 238, 282, 290, 295

Middlemarch by George Eliot
Issues: 210, 356, 483, 452, 472

Persuasion by Jane Austen
Issues: 241, 337, 348, 423, 459

The Quest for Corvo: An Experiment in Biography by A.J.A. Symons
Issues: 174, 177, 280, 377, 509

The Sword of Honour Trilogy by Evelyn Waugh
Issues: 187, 226, 245, 348, 449, 476

Three Men in a Boat by Jerome K. Jerome
Issues: 31, 114, 118, 370, 474

Vile Bodies by Evelyn Waugh
Issues: 32, 41, 302, 310, 392

100 Years of Solitude by Gabriel Garcia Marquez
Issues: 202, 261, 265, 367

American Pastoral by Philip Roth
Issues: 262, 308, 344, 526,

Barchester Towers by Anthony Trollope
Issues: 47, 144, 215, 442

Cold Comfort Farm by Stella Gibbons
Issues: 246, 304, 339, 469

Decline and Fall by Evelyn Waugh
Issues: 54, 154, 250, 444

Diaries by Alan Clark
Issues: 105, 118, 306, 511

Disraeli by Robert Blake
Issues: 160, 217, 260. 263

Herzog by Saul Bellow
Issues: 205, 208, 483, 516

Kim by Rudyard Kipling
Issues: 135, 187, 214, 281

Madame Bovary by Gustave Flaubert
Issues: 298, 341, 428, 365

Quartered Safe Out Here by George MacDonald Fraser
Issues: 214, 234, 286, 512,

The Big Sleep by Raymond Chandler
Issues: 123, 252, 264, 278

The Catcher in the Rye by J.D. Salinger
Issues: 189, 195, 292, 438

The Code of the Woosters by P.G. Wodehouse
Issues: 301, 336, 442, 486

The Last Chronicles of Barset by Anthony Trollope
Issues: 54, 250, 375, 529

The Master and Margarita by Mikhail Bulgakov
Issues: 261, 291, 302, 375,

The Pursuit of Love by Nancy Mitford
Issues: 237, 422, 478, 520

To Kill a Mockingbird by Harper Lee
Issues: 295, 348, 457, 477

Treasure Island by R.L. Stevenson
Issues: 338, 415, 444, 477

Space limitations prevent us from publishing a full list of the 36 books that qualified for Ninth place with 3 votes each, and the 90 books that received 2 votes apiece, bringing them into Tenth place.

The World's Top Authors

Position	Votes	
1	45	**Evelyn Waugh**

Scoop 14, Brideshead Revisited 6,
The Sword of Honour 6, Decline and Fall 4,
Vile Bodies 4, A Handful of Dust 3,
Put Out More Flags 2, A Little Learning 1,
Scott-King's Modern Europe 1,
The Great Gilbert Pinfold 1,
The Loved One 1, The Letters of Evelyn
Waugh 1, Men At Arms Trilogy 1

Position	Votes	
2=	25	**P G Wodehouse**

Code of the Woosters 4, The Inimitable
Jeeves 3, Blandings Castle 2,
The Mating Season 2, Jeeves & The
Feudal Spirit 2, Full Moon 1,
Joy in the Morning 1, Right Ho, Jeeves 1,
The Jeeves Omnibus 1,The Oldest
Member 1, Very Good, Jeeves 1,
Gold Omnibus Stories 1, Mike and
Psmith 1, The Luck of the Bodkins 1,
Mulliner Nights 1, Summer Lightning 1,
Heavy Weather 1

Position	Votes	
2=	25	**Charles Dickens**

Great Expectations 7, Pickwick Papers 3,
A Christmas Carol 2, A Tale of Two Cities 2,
Little Dorrit 2, Our Mutual Friend 3,
Bleak House 2, Pictures from Italy 1,
Dombey and Son 1, Nicholas Nickleby 1,
The Old Curiosity Shop 1

Position	Votes	
4	17	**Jane Austen**

Emma 5, Persuasion 5,
Pride and Prejudice 5, Mansfield Park 1,
Northanger Abbey 1

Position	Votes	
6	15	**Anthony Trollope**

Barchester Towers 5, The Last Chronicle
of Barset 4, Framley Parsonage 2,
Orley Farm 2, The Way We Live Now 2
The Small House at Allington 1,
The Warden 1, Phineas Finn 1
The Chronicles of Barsetshire 1,
The Eustace Diamond 1, The Prime
Minister 1

Position	Votes	
7	8	**William Shakespeare**

King Lear 2, Shakespeare's Sonnets 2,
Twelfth Night 2, A Midsummer Night's
Dream 1, Henry 1V parts 1 and 2, and
Henry V1

And just to be different, the World's Worst Books... chosen by seven leading writers

The BBC ran a nationwide poll to discover our favourite books. In contrast, The Independent asked leading literary figures to name the novels they think most overrated.

Matthew Parris, journalist and Conservative MP: *Swallows and Amazons* by Arthur Ransome (Red Fox). I found it infuriating as a child, as it was extraordinarily well written but nothing ever happened. I was always waiting for some kind of plot to emerge.

Joan Smith, author: *Possession* by A.S. Byatt (Vintage). It's a kind of schmaltzy Mills & Boon romance dressed up with cod Victorian poetry to make it seem more profound. It has no emotional depth at all, but is incredibly shallow and trivial.

Carmen Callil, publisher and founder of Virago Books: *The God of Small Things* by Arundhati Roy (Flamingo). This novel combines total lack of originality with romantic, twittering prose.

J.G. Ballard, author: *Finnegan's Wake* by James Joyce (Penguin). This incomprehensible novel repre-sents a lamentable tendency in 20th century fiction: the quest for total obscurity. Finnegan's Wake is the best example of modernism disappearing up its own fundament.

John Walsh, author and columnist: *The Lord of the Rings* by J.R.R. Tolkien (HarperCollins). For inspiring life-long loathing, nothing beats The Lord of the Rings. The childish storytelling, the valetudinarian mythologising, Tolkein's lack of feel for language, landscape or emotion; the desire to garrotte Pippin and Merry in a dark alley – how can so many readers have put up with such codswallop for so long?

Blake Morrison, author and literary critic: *Jonathan Livingstone Seagull* by Richard Bach (HarperCollins). It's a self-important parable and complete piffle.

P.D. James, author: *Rebecca* by Daphne du Maurier (Arrow). I find Max de Winter deeply unsympathetic. He's arrogant, bullying and insensitive. Surely he must have realised that his young, inexperienced bride couldn't cope with Mrs Danvers?

Issue 410: 24th May 2003